T0163634

OUR PEACEFUL PLANET

OUR PEACEFUL PLANET

Healing Ourselves and Our World
for a Sustainable Future

YASMIN DAVAR

NEW YORK

NASHVILLE • MELBOURNE • VANCOUVER

OUR PEACEFUL PLANET
Healing Ourselves and Our World for a Sustainable Future

© 2017 YASMIN DAVAR

All rights reserved. No portion of this book may be reproduced, stored in a retrieval system, or transmitted in any form or by any means—electronic, mechanical, photocopy, recording, scanning, or other,—except for brief quotations in critical reviews or articles, without the prior written permission of the publisher.

Published in New York, New York, by Morgan James Publishing. Morgan James and The Entrepreneurial Publisher are trademarks of Morgan James, LLC. www.MorganJamesPublishing.com

The Morgan James Speakers Group can bring authors to your live event. For more information or to book an event visit The Morgan James Speakers Group at www.TheMorganJamesSpeakersGroup.com.

ISBN 978-1-68350-240-1 paperback
ISBN 978-1-68350-242-5 eBook
ISBN 978-1-68350-241-8 hardcover
Library of Congress Control Number: 2016915420

Cover Design by:
Rachel Lopez
www.r2cdesign.com

Interior Design by:
Bonnie Bushman
The Whole Caboodle Graphic Design

In an effort to support local communities, raise awareness and funds, Morgan James Publishing donates a percentage of all book sales for the life of each book to Habitat for Humanity Peninsula and Greater Williamsburg.

Get involved today! Visit
www.MorganJamesBuilds.com

CONTENTS

PREFACE

My hope is that the ideas contained in these pages inspire you to think differently about yourself, the people in your world, and the world we live in. Beyond that, I hope your changed perceptions compel you to approach your life, the lives of others, and the earth in ways that lead to greater harmony, love, and respect.

Introduction

THE CASE FOR CHANGE

The Chernobyl disaster of April 26, 1986 had an incredible impact on my twelve-year-old self. What a terrible thing to happen, devastating the lives of many people and impacting the environment for many years to come. The Cold War was in full flight at the time, and every day on the news we heard about the latest nuclear arms build-up and posturing between the United States and the former Soviet Union. Even at that young age, I thought that there must be a better way to do things. Surely we do not need to be so unkind to each other and rely on technologies that ravage the environment?

This question has led me, through a degree in Environmental Engineering and another in International Relations in Peace and Conflict Resolution, through work in both fields and in the corporate world, to the ideas that are contained in this book.

I am not sure that we have progressed far since that accident in 1986. While we have had major breakthroughs with the end of the Cold War and the dismantling of apartheid, as I write this, conflicts are being fought in Syria and Iraq, and Israel and Palestine still have not come to a resolution. Many people are denied the right to choose their leaders, and millions live in poverty despite the enormous wealth in the world. The 2011 Fukushima nuclear power plant disaster in Japan will have social and environmental impacts for years to come. Rainforests in Asia and South America are being destroyed for the production of palm oil and beef. The effects of climate change are being felt by people and ecosystems across the world.

Is this the way we want to keep going? I am by no means suggesting an apocalyptic end to the world with a massive world war and our environment completely ravaged by our endless consumerism. What I see, and many of you see as well, is a gradual (and sometimes not gradual) decline in the well-being of many people and the environment. Where will we find ourselves at the end of this decline, and will this be where we want to be?

Rather than blindly sliding down that slippery slope, let's assume that we have control over the outcome. If we could choose what our planet looks like in ten, twenty, or fifty years' time, what would we choose? I believe that the most popular answer would be a world where we live in peace and harmony with each other and our environment, where the well-being of all living things is high.

Some might say that this world is a fantasy. I disagree. This world is completely within our reach, and this book sets out what we can do to realize it. It covers how we can consciously change our beliefs and behaviors, and what modifications we can make to existing governance, industrial, and economic systems to enable greater harmony, equality, and well-being.

You may think that you, as only one person, can have little impact on the world. This is not true. Many of us work in areas where we can influence change at local, national, and international levels. Many of us work in industries that are not as kind to the environment as they could be. A great many of us can influence the behavior of governments and corporations through both our voting and purchasing power. And all of us have the power to change our own beliefs and behaviors. This is the greatest power of all, and is where we will start.

PART 1

HEALING
OURSELVES

HEALING FROM
THE INSIDE OUT

Given the opportunity, most of us would welcome the chance to live happier and more meaningful lives. It naturally follows that if we want the world to be a happier place and for people to live in peace, then each of us needs to be happier and more at peace within ourselves. This is because we project everything we have inside of us out into the world. Both pain and happiness ripple out from us in direct proportion to the amounts of each that we carry inside. This is why change starts with each of us first, even though it may seem that changes in others, or at a national or international level, are more important.

It's easy to blame others — our parents, our partner, our boss, the government, or people from another country or group — for things that seem outside of our control. We sometimes overlook the part we play in our everyday interactions. We forget how much power each of us has in shaping our own lives, the lives of those around us, and the world in which we live. The way we react to situations, the roles we play, the choices we make, and whether we take responsibility for these things, all directly shape our world.

Change in the world can only happen when each of us takes responsibility for our impact on the world. It is up to each of us to heal our internal pain and the negative beliefs behind that pain, so that more peace and happiness ripple out from within. In this way, we can then live in greater harmony with ourselves and those around us. The increased happiness in the world provides a stronger foundation to make the changes that are required in our global society, as shown in Figure 1.

Figure 1:
Our peaceful planet is created by positive change at both the individual and societal levels.

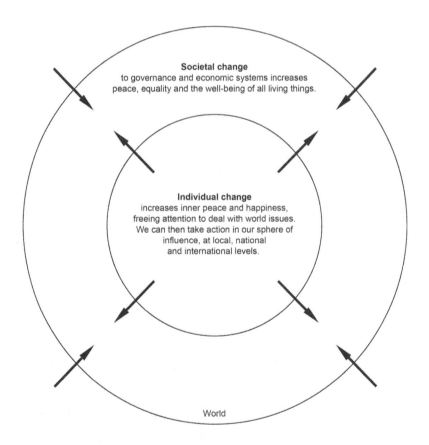

Societal change
to governance and economic systems increases
peace, equality and the well-being of all living things.

Individual change
increases inner peace and happiness,
freeing attention to deal with world issues.
We can then take action in our sphere of
influence, at local, national
and international levels.

World

The exercises in the first three chapters of this book are designed to help you heal and be the best person you can be. Please take this opportunity to do them so you can begin creating a happier and more meaningful life for yourself. They are designed to help you quickly and easily identify your core negative beliefs and heal them.

Even if you do not feel you have major issues in your life that need resolving, it is useful to run through each of the exercises at least once to get a feel for them, and to understand how they work by doing them. You will find that some of your hurt has gone, and you have discovered new things about yourself. Once you are familiar with the exercises, you can return to do the ones that you feel will best help you in your life. Being familiar with the exercises on a personal level also helps those working in group reconciliation to achieve the best results.

We don't need to wait until we have healed all of our pain and negative beliefs before we start working on the changes that are outlined in Part 2 of this book. But the more we heal, the more we realize how amazing we are, and the more we can achieve together. Let's start.

The Impact of Pain

Most of us have some level of unresolved pain within us. The more we have, the more likely we are to create a series of negative experiences and to do things that cause other people to feel pain too. In this way, each of us projects our pain out into the world. As we heal, we reduce the need to hurt others to get what we want, or to feel better about ourselves. This in turn reduces the amount of pain being spread across the earth, and increases the flow of happiness.

Most unresolved pain and anger is linked to traumatic events in our lives. Most of us have been affected in some way by dysfunctional families, relationship breakups, divorce, peer rejection, serious illness, or the death of loved ones. Some of us have lived through abuse, others through war. There is no denying that these events are painful. Many of us have not had the tools or support to process our pain, so we repress these experiences and the accompanying feelings inside of ourselves.

The pain inside you increases every time you have a negative experience and decreases when you heal from one. Some people hold the repressed pain from only one or two experiences inside themselves. Others hold the repressed pain from everything that has ever happened to them. Some people's pain is so overwhelming they develop addictive behaviors to try to block it out.

Some people believe they can control their pain by keeping it pushed down inside of them. We like to fool ourselves into thinking that everything is okay to avoid dealing with pain. But the truth is that our pain increases and boils over whenever we hit a new bump in life. It is amplified in new situations and inhibits our ability to manage those situations rationally. Our pain also boils over when our ability to stay in control is compromised — like when we are angry, under pressure, or have had alcohol or drugs. We then project our pain onto other people in our lives — whether or not we intend for that to happen — hurting them and giving us cause to regret our actions. This of course, only increases the amount of pain we hold inside. The only way to truly be in control of your pain is to heal it.

Let's look at one example of how pain affects your life. Imagine your partner cheated on you. You would feel very hurt and question whether you can ever trust them or anyone else again. If you don't heal and move to a place of forgiveness, then at least one of four things is likely to happen. The first is that you develop addictive behaviors to dull the pain. You may drink more than you used to, or overeat, or any number of other harmful behaviors. The second is that you are too scared to enter into a new relationship, thereby denying yourself the chance of happiness with another person. The third is that you carry your pain into your next relationship and project it onto your new partner. Because you are viewing your new partner through the lens of your pain, you may not see them for the trustworthy person they are, and wrongfully accuse them of infidelity. The fourth is that you attract a new partner who cheats on you too. The more pain you hold inside, the less likely you are to handle these situations well, and you may find yourself adding to your pain.

Why do these things happen?

We feel pain every time we go through a negative experience, and we attract negative experiences as a result of the negative beliefs we hold about ourselves and our world. Most of our beliefs are formed during childhood, usually by the time we are four years old. Negative beliefs are also formed during traumatic experiences. In the example, the experience of being cheated on has created negative beliefs about yourself and what it means to be in a relationship. You then negatively shape the world around you and create more pain with these beliefs. It is therefore critical that we understand what beliefs we hold so we can heal our pain and shape our world in positive ways.

Understanding Beliefs

Let's start with a definition. What is a *belief*? It is an idea that you hold to be true.[1] Many people do not think they shape the world around them through the beliefs they hold. They have difficulty comprehending that they have such an impact on their lives, their futures, and their world. An alternate and commonly held view is that your experiences in your world form your beliefs (not the other way around), or "you believe it when you see it."[2] This is a limiting approach, making you a passive victim of circumstance. Rather than shaping the world around you, you are allowing yourself to be shaped by it.[3]

Some people deny that their beliefs shape the world around them because otherwise they would have to take responsibility for everything in their life, both good and bad. No one is perfect, and we have all had times when we've looked back on our lives and become despondent about the negative things we have created.

Taking responsibility for your beliefs and your subsequent actions is the most important step in the healing process. Deny this, and you deny yourself the ability to bring good things into your life. This is because your ability to create both good and bad in your life is one and the same — it is the belief that you hold that determines the outcome.

Remember that a belief is an idea that you hold to be true. Acknowledging that your beliefs form the world around you puts you in a powerful position, because you have the ability to change what you hold to be true, and transform your life in positive and loving ways. This transformation affects your life and the people around you, demonstrating your individual power to create change in the world.

Before we heal our negative beliefs, it's important to understand what our beliefs are based on and how this affects us. Positive beliefs are based on three important principles: *inclusion, deservedness,* and *abundance*:

- *Inclusion* means that you belong and are connected to a greater whole.
- *Deservedness* means that you are worthy.
- *Abundance* means that there is plenty of something to go around.

People who are successful in one or more areas of their life — with a loving family, financial good fortune, or thriving careers — have created this for themselves by believing that they belong in the world and deserve to have these good things which are available to everyone through the abundance of the universe. Importantly, they haven't placed fear-based limits on themselves or the way in which their success comes to them. They have merely allowed it to manifest in their lives.

Negative beliefs are based on the opposite principles: *separateness, undeservedness,* and *lack*:

- *Separateness* means that you are disconnected from others and a greater whole.
- *Undeservedness* means that you are not worthy.
- *Lack* means that there is not enough of something to go around.

People who are unsuccessful in one or more areas of their lives have created this by believing that they are separate from or different than everyone else, they don't deserve to have good things, and there are not enough good things to go around for everyone anyway. You may know some people whose negative beliefs completely rule every aspect of their lives. Most of us, however, struggle with just one or two aspects of our lives like our career, health, or our love life.

Holding negative beliefs about ourselves leads alternatively to aggression and victimhood. Regardless of the outcome, we all lose because we struggle and separate ourselves from the universal flow of life. The reality is that there is no separateness, undeservedness, or lack. It is only our belief in these things that causes the world to appear so.

You, me, and that group of people over there; the plants, animals, and minerals; everything on earth and throughout the universe — we are all one. We are all made up of the same basic matter and energy which we exchange freely with each other and the rest of the universe. Each of us has divine life force flowing through us and all of the abundance of the universe is readily available for us to create all of the wonderful things that we desire. Each one of us is a beautiful soul who deserves to have peace, love, and prosperity in our lives.

When we approach our life with this foundation of inclusion, deservedness, and abundance, our beliefs about ourselves and our relationships change. We want the best for ourselves and those around us, because with the abundance of the universe this is possible. Our relationships improve because we exercise greater compassion for ourselves and others. We joyfully create peace and happiness in our lives. We no longer need to be externally validated, because we understand our innate perfection and that of everyone and everything else. Inner peace replaces inner struggle.

Let's consider our individual beliefs and the impact they have on our lives, so we can start healing, and get to this place of inner peace. An easy way to recognize the beliefs you hold is to look for repeating patterns in your life. Consider first the good things that you have. It may be loving relationships, good friends, and work you enjoy. You can probably remember your success in something, like a sport, artistic talent, or your work. Some common beliefs you may hold to create this success include:

- My family and friends love me and treat me with respect.
- I have everything I need.
- I am good at a particular thing, for example: soccer, or singing, or trivia, or bricklaying, or finance, or surgery.
- I can succeed at whatever task I attempt.

Try identifying the positive things you have in your life, and the beliefs you hold which have created these positive things. Consider how these things are based on inclusion, deservedness, and abundance. A loving relationship, for example, is based on belonging with someone else, believing that you deserve to be loved, and that there is romantic love for you in the world. A successful career is based on finding the best way for you to contribute to the world, and believing that you deserve to be successful, your contribution is important, and that success is available to everyone.

Now let's turn to the more painful repeating patterns in your life. They may be broken relationships, conflict with family members or colleagues, or problems managing your finances. Some beliefs you may hold which create conflict in your life include:

- It's always someone else's fault, not mine.
- Good things never happen to me.
- I am not loved or treated with respect.
- There isn't enough to go around.

Consider how these beliefs are based on separateness, undeservedness, and lack, and how they impact our lives. For example, people who always blame others hold themselves separate from others and frequently don't have many friends. Those who believe that good things never happen to them perpetuate this belief by choosing the worst available options. They do so because they don't believe they deserve better for themselves. People who repeatedly choose partners who control them or conversely neglect them don't believe they deserve to be loved and treated with respect. Those who believe that there isn't enough to go around manifest this by frittering away their money, because they don't believe they deserve to participate in the abundance of the universe. You can easily recognize these behaviors in both yourself and those around you, because these are beliefs we all hold to some extent. Because we believe these negative beliefs are true, we repeatedly undertake destructive actions.

Consider the impact that holding negative beliefs has on your life. The pain you hold inside you dims your inner light. You hurt yourself and others over and over again. Healing your negative beliefs is easier than lugging all that pain around for the rest of your life. There doesn't have to be a place inside of you that always hurts or that you avoid. You can have a happier life, and let your inner light shine.

Healing Negative Beliefs

Everyone has within them *life force*, that inexplicable energy that keeps us alive. This life force flows through the universe, through our planet, and through each of us. It is pure and powerful. Regardless of what you may think of yourself, or how much you may doubt yourself, this pure, strong, and unchanging force flows through you until the moment you die.

Close your eyes, be still for a moment, and feel your life force flowing through you. Imagine your life force as a light and see this light flowing through every cell of your body. We are going to use this force and the wisdom of our bodies to heal our pain and negative beliefs. Earlier, we discussed how we repress painful experiences and emotions inside ourselves. As we do this, they become locked as a memory in the cells of our body. Nothing is forgotten. Our body has its own intelligence. It is amazing — we breathe, digest food, grow hair, and replenish our cells without ever having to think about it. This same intelligence helps us access our cellular memories and heal.

Healing can be done on your own or with a trusted partner to guide you through the steps. Some of you have experienced abuse, and while you know it has had an incredibly negative impact on your life and the way you view yourself, you may be scared to face it. You do not need to be. Trust your body's innate wisdom. Know that with that powerful life force flowing through you, you are stronger than you think. You deserve to be free, happy, and whole.

You may find that your fear exhibits itself through a reluctance to admit you are holding negative beliefs. You get the best results from this exercise when you are very honest with yourself and willing to go to the core of your painful, negative experiences. Don't judge or beat yourself up. Just allow what comes up to come up, and follow the steps to heal it:

1. Sit in a quiet space where you are unlikely to be distracted. You need to concentrate for the duration of the exercise. Identify a painful situation

in your life where you struggle or have struggled, and which may have occurred repeatedly. It may be a problem with relationships, your health, your finances, or your career.

2. Allow yourself to feel the emotional response associated with this situation. You may feel pain in your heart or stomach area. Some people have blocked their pain for so long that they don't feel anything. If this is the case for you, deliberately shift your awareness to your heart or stomach area — whichever you think is best — and lift the lid off your pain. Then allow yourself to drop into the pain so you can feel it.

3. Don't get caught up in the story of the situation that caused the pain. Just picture or feel this pain as a black ball, and surround it with the light of your life force. Your life force creates a sacred space within you where only truth is told.

4. Place your awareness in the black ball of pain and ask your body what belief you hold to have caused this experience or series of experiences, and when that belief was formed.

5. Be very still and wait for the answer to form in your consciousness. It sounds different than the normal chatter of your mind. It is profound and to the point. You may "hear" what the belief you hold is in your mind. Sometimes you may also "see" a picture of a person or an event linked to the formation of the negative belief. Accompanying this may be a reenactment of how the negative belief was formed that offers a wider perspective of that experience. Allow whatever you hear or see to play out, as though you are listening to the radio or watching TV. You find your belief was formed either when you were young or during a traumatic event.

6. If a person appeared in relation to the formation of your negative belief, ask them why they acted the way they did. In the light of your life force, their answer is honest and direct. You may ask clarifying questions, but keep the dialogue short and direct. The purpose is to get to the heart of the matter without obscuring it with unnecessary talk and questions.

7. Usually, this person says they are sorry for the way they acted. Even if they do not, it is necessary to exercise compassion and understanding in

order for you to heal. Tell them that you forgive them, and do so from the heart. It is more powerful if you say it out loud. You may also choose to thank them for any positive things they have contributed to your life.

8. If a person or an event does not appear, ask your body what is required to heal the negative belief. Wait for an answer to form in your consciousness. Sometimes it is necessary to simply forgive ourselves for holding the negative belief and putting ourselves through a series of traumatic experiences. Once again, it is more powerful if we forgive ourselves from the heart, out loud.

9. Burn through your ball of pain with the light of your life force. Then extend your light into every cell of your body to remove the negative belief.

10. Return your awareness to your heart or stomach area and ask your body what positive belief you can create to bring happiness into your life. Your body responds with a positive belief based on inclusion, deservedness, and abundance. Allow it to form in your consciousness. Once again, it is profound and to the point.

11. Cradle this positive belief and wrap the light of your life force around it. Then extend the light of your life force into every cell in your body to embed this positive belief. You may experience a series of positive realizations through this process. Enjoy them — they are a lovely part of the healing process.

We can consider how this healing exercise works by returning to the example of the cheating partner. Perhaps this partner is not the first to cheat on you or neglect you in some way. You may hold yourself separate from others, and feel undeserving of the love and happiness which is lacking in your life. Hold the pain associated with this experience in a black ball and surround it with the light of your life force. Place your awareness in the black ball of pain. Ask your body what belief you hold to have caused this experience, and when that belief was formed. You may discover that you believe you don't deserve to be loved. This belief may have formed during a traumatic relationship breakdown or abusive event in your past.

In the dialogue with the other person involved, they may explain that the way they treated you was a result of a traumatic event that they themselves experienced as a child, and from which they did not heal. They ask for your forgiveness. Forgive them and burn through the negative belief with the light of your life force, removing it from every cell of your body. Ask your body what positive belief you can hold. The response may be: *I am loved.* State your new, positive belief in the present tense to demonstrate that you are included, deserving, and that it flows to you through the abundance of the universe. Use the light of your life force to embed this belief into the cells of your body, and you are healed.

Let's try another example. Perhaps you are having difficulty getting ahead in your career. Maybe you feel you have no direction in life and have flitted from job to job. In doing this exercise, you may discover that you believe you will not be accepted by your friends and family if you are successful, or that you don't deserve to be successful. This belief may have formed in childhood when you heard negative messages about wealthy people, or when you were told you were dumb. After forgiving yourself and anyone else involved in the formation of your negative belief, and burning through it with the light of your life force, you may replace the negative belief with a positive belief such as, *I am accepted as I am* or, *I am successful.*

You usually feel lighter and freer after conducting this exercise. If you don't, it may be because you did not trust your body's wisdom, or perhaps you had difficulty fully forgiving. Let a bit of time pass and then do the exercise again. You may then be at a different stage of your personal development and more ready to face your pain. Put what you think to one side, allow yourself to listen to your body, and be really honest. Remember not to judge yourself. You are taking steps to heal and should be proud of yourself.

By healing your negative beliefs, you break negative repeating patterns and manifest better situations in your life. This is because you change the way you perceive a person or situation through the healing process, and that person or situation changes in response. Sometimes this happens without you saying or doing anything more than the healing.

By accepting responsibility for your part in the situation and changing the belief you held that created it, you are able to think of yourself, anyone else involved, and what has occurred, with more compassion. Your interactions with the other people involved, if they are still in your life, improve. New opportunities reflecting your new beliefs appear.

It is up to you to consciously address the negative beliefs you hold and direct the change you want in your life. Keep doing the healing exercise until all the pain inside of you is gone, and you are more peaceful and joyful. Happiness ripples out from you every time you heal. In this way, each shift in your beliefs, no matter how large or small, is important in creating a happier and more peaceful world.

୬ Key Messages ଜ

- Reducing the pain and increasing the happiness in each of us provides a better foundation to make the changes that are required in our global society.
- You shape the world around you through the beliefs you hold.
- A happy and peaceful world is created through positive beliefs based on inclusion, deservedness, and abundance.

POWER, IDENTITY,
AND RELATIONSHIPS

W hile pain and repeating patterns are the most obvious ways to identify the impact of negative beliefs in our lives, there are two other indicators — the use of power and the use of identity. We use these two concepts because we feel powerless and worthless inside, and it temporarily makes us feel better. In reality, the use of power and identity is underpinned by our negative beliefs, and they perpetuate separateness, undeservedness, and lack in our lives and the lives of those around us. As such, they are the cause of great unhappiness throughout the world. Addressing the use of power and identity is the next step in our healing journey.

Healing the negative beliefs underpinning the use of power and identity is one of the most powerful things you can do for yourself and those around you. It results in greater inner peace, strength, and belonging. This provides us with a much stronger basis to build happy and peaceful lives, and create harmony and well-being in the world around us.

The majority of the steps of the exercises in this chapter are the same as those in the previous exercise for healing beliefs. They are repeated here because the entry into healing is different in each case. Let's continue healing.

The Use of Power

We have all been brought up to believe that to win and be perceived as strong is good, to lose or be perceived as weak is bad. The unfortunate impact of this belief is that, for many of us, we have to win and be acknowledged as being the best over and over again in order to feel good about ourselves. Without power, we feel hollow, worthless, separate from the world, and undeserving of love and respect.

This leads to the repetition of destructive behavior, which some of us are prepared to carry out without thought to the impact on others. This behavior includes:

- the pursuit of money and prestige
- endless competition
- physical and emotional abuse to dominate others
- unethical and illegal actions, such as lying, tax evasion, robbery, and other crimes
- thinking that we are better or smarter than everyone else
- an inability to compromise for fear of appearing weak and
- sulking until we get what we want.

Many people have discovered that all of their wealth and power has not made them happy. Others have lost the respect of colleagues and peers because they haven't been ethical in their dealings with them. Some expend a lot of energy trying to prove they are right or the best at everything, only to lose friends. Others distance themselves to punish their loved ones, only to end up alone. A good number have won the argument, only to lose the relationship.

The use of power frequently results in broken relationships, anger, and regret — for both the person exercising power and for those around them — leaving trails of unhappiness through the world. When we exercise power over others, all we are doing is demonstrating our negative beliefs based on separateness, undeservedness, and lack. Power is a temporary high that does not bring long-term happiness or acceptance of self. This is because personal wellbeing is independent of power. A person does not have to be powerful in the traditional sense of the word to be happy.

Healing the Use of Power

Healing requires identifying the negative beliefs we are feeding through the use of power, and acknowledging that we don't need to continue exerting power in this negative way to feel good about ourselves. We feel genuinely good about ourselves when we love and accept ourselves, and recognize how beautiful we are. With this foundation, we can create wonderful things in our lives because we deserve them.

Once again, you get the best results when you are very honest with yourself, and willing to go to the core of your painful, negative experiences. Don't judge or beat yourself up. Just allow what comes up to come up, and follow the steps to heal it:

1. Sit in a quiet space where you can concentrate and identify the ways in which you exercise power over others. Considering the repeating patterns in your life helps. Remember that most of our beliefs are formed when we are very young and are influenced by our experiences with our parents or other people in positions of power. You may find that your relationship with power mimics the way they used power, or has developed in direct response to the way they used power.

2. Allow yourself to feel the emotional response associated with this situation. You may feel pain in your heart or stomach area. Some people have blocked their pain for so long that they don't feel anything. If this is the case for you, shift your awareness to your heart or stomach area — whichever you think is best — and lift the lid off your pain. Then allow yourself to drop into the pain so that you can feel it.

3. Don't get caught up in the story of the situation that caused the pain. Just picture or feel this pain as a black ball, and surround it with the light of your life force. Your life force creates a sacred space within you where only truth is told.

4. Place your awareness in the black ball of pain and ask your body what belief you hold that caused this use of power, and when that belief was formed.

5. Be very still and wait for the answer to form in your consciousness. It sounds different than the normal chatter of your mind. It is profound and to the point. You may "hear" what the belief you hold is in your mind. Sometimes you may also "see" a picture of a person or an event linked to the formation of the negative belief. Accompanying this may be a reenactment of how the negative belief was formed that offers a wider perspective of that experience. Allow whatever you hear or see to play out, as though you are listening to the radio or watching TV. You find your belief was formed either when you were young or during a traumatic event.

6. If a person appeared in relation to the formation of your negative belief, ask them why they acted the way they did. In the light of your life force, their answer is honest and direct. You may ask clarifying questions, but keep the dialogue short and direct. The purpose is to get to the heart of the matter without obscuring it with unnecessary talk and questions.

7. Usually, this person says they are sorry for the way they acted. Even if they do not, it is necessary to exercise compassion and understanding in order for you to heal. Tell them that you forgive them, and do so from the heart. It is more powerful if you say it out loud. You may also choose to thank them for any positive things they have contributed to your life.

8. If a person or an event does not appear, ask your body what is required to heal the negative belief. Wait for an answer to form in your consciousness. Sometimes it is necessary to simply forgive ourselves for holding the negative belief, and putting ourselves through a series of traumatic experiences. Once again, it is more powerful if we forgive ourselves from the heart, out loud.

9. Burn through your ball of pain with the light of your life force. Then extend your light into every cell of your body to remove the negative belief.

10. Return your awareness to your heart or stomach area, and ask your body what positive belief you can create to bring happiness into your life. Your body responds with a positive belief based on inclusion, deservedness,

and abundance. Allow it to form in your consciousness. Once again, it is profound and to the point.

11. Cradle this positive belief and wrap the light of your life force around it. Then extend the light of your life force into every cell in your body to embed this positive belief. You may experience a series of positive realizations through this process. Enjoy them — they are a lovely part of the healing process.

For example, perhaps you like to win arguments and competitions. You fight hard for recognition and acceptance, and dominate others to get it. You feel separate or different from others, and undeserving of having recognition and acceptance flow to you. Hold the pain associated with this experience in a black ball and surround it with the light of your life force. Focus your awareness on the black ball of pain. Ask your body what belief you hold that causes this use of power, and when that belief was formed. You may discover that you believe you don't deserve recognition and acceptance for just being who you are. This belief may have formed in childhood when you felt you had to be the best to gain a parent's approval or attention.

In the dialogue with your parent, they may tell you that their attention was placed on struggling to maintain their relationship with their spouse, or on making ends meet — both manifestations of negative beliefs that they themselves have not healed. They ask for your forgiveness. Forgive them and burn through the negative belief with the light of your life force, removing it from every cell of your body. Ask your body what positive belief you can hold. The response may be: *I am recognized and accepted as I am.* State your new, positive belief in the present tense to demonstrate that you are included, and deserving, and that it flows to you through the abundance of the universe. Use the light of your life force to embed this belief into the cells of your body, and you are healed.

Let's try another example. Perhaps you lie, cheat, or steal. You may have grown up in a poor household and not liked sharing things with your siblings, or you may be following the example set by your parents. You may tell yourself that lying, cheating, or stealing is the only way to get what you want, and that you deserve the spoils of your activities, even if other people suffer in order for you to have them. You feel separate from others and undeserving of good things, which don't flow into your life. Through the exercise, you may discover that you really believe that you do not deserve to have good things in your life. After forgiving yourself and anyone else involved in the formation of this negative belief, and burning through it with the light of your life force, you may replace the negative belief with a positive one, such as: *Good things flow to me through the abundance of the universe*, or *I have good things in my life*.

Once you heal the beliefs which underpin your use of power, you no longer undertake these destructive actions. Healing the use of power is incredibly freeing. It enables you to remember your innate perfection, and thus love and accept yourself as you are. It creates inner strength and inner peace. All the attention and energy you used to create and maintain power can now be used to expand your life in ways that bring about greater happiness and well-being to yourself and others.

It's time to redefine power. To have inner peace and spread that peace throughout the world, *that* is power.

The Use of Identity

Now let's turn to the use of identity. We use identity to create certainty for ourselves and meaning in our lives. This is who I am. This is where I belong. This is what I represent. While we think the use of identity makes us whole, it actually separates us from others and restricts us from being everything we can be.

The easiest way to identify identities is to consider the roles we play in our lives. We allow our identity to be defined by our position in our family, or by more general roles such as a rebel or a princess, a rescuer or a failure. Most commonly, we define our identity by our profession. For many of us, what we do mistakenly becomes who we are. I am a plumber, or an academic, or a dentist, or a soldier. We attach our self-worth to our profession because some of us believe our jobs are one of the few things we do well in life, or the only area in our lives where we are appreciated.

For some of us, the use of our professional identity is linked with the use of power. But what happens if someone else doesn't think we are as good at our jobs as we do? Or if in this world of rapid movement within and between professions, we are expected to change our role within the place where we work? Because we have defined ourselves so narrowly, our confidence plummets. We lose sight of the fact that we can acquire the skills to become competent in other jobs because we have based our lives on the idea that we are one thing, and therefore cannot be another.

We may also define our identity by our role as parents. Parenting is an all-consuming role. We receive a lot of validation from our children who shower us with love, especially when they are young. As children become teens, they may develop different ideas about life than their parents and distance themselves in order to define their own identities. Children also eventually leave home in the natural progression of life. People who define themselves by their parenting role require constant validation from their children to continue to feel good about themselves. These people lose their confidence in themselves and their connection to the world when the relationship with their children changes, because they have defined themselves so narrowly.

The adoption of family identities can result in a repetition of beliefs and behaviors across generations. For example, those who believe they come from a long line of hardworking men and women who earn little become trapped by their use of identity. While it gives them a sense of belonging, it also restricts their ability to lift themselves out of poverty. Similarly, those who come from a long line of "no hopers" trap themselves in cycles of failure, because they do not believe that they deserve and can achieve wonderful things in their lives.

Some identities are created out of our experiences as children within our families. For example, those who have provided emotional support to a parent as a child, perhaps because their parent is sick or not coping after a relationship breakdown, frequently continue to play the same role as adults. They repeatedly choose partners or friends who need to be rescued and looked after.

While the act of rescuing gives a feeling of belonging and purpose, those being rescued may not appreciate the support, and may return to their destructive behaviors. Rescuers often fall into a pattern of being hurt by the people they are trying to save. Similarly, those who were spoiled as children often look for partners who can afford to continue to spoil them, without properly considering that it is their compatibility with their partners that determines their future happiness, rather than material possessions.

Using identities makes us feel whole by giving us the things we want — belonging, appreciation, confidence, compassion from others, or when combined with the use of power, our own way. However, the key outcome of using identities is that it separates us from others and restricts us.

We seek to define ourselves by what we are good at, who we belong with, and how we are different from others. But for everything we say we are, there are many very good people and things that we exclude ourselves from. Everyone uses identities. No matter which identities we choose, they are another way of playing out the negative beliefs we hold based on separateness, undeservedness, and lack.

Healing the Use of Identity

Healing involves identifying the negative belief we are feeding through the use of identities, and acknowledging that we don't need to continue using the identity to create positive things in our lives. With the abundance of the universe at our disposal, we can create positive things because we deserve them.

Let's take a moment to deconstruct the identities we have created for ourselves, and heal the negative beliefs underpinning them. Once again, you get the best outcome when you are very honest with yourself, and willing to go to the core of your painful, negative experiences. Don't judge or beat yourself up. Just allow what comes up to come up, and follow the steps to heal it:

1. Sit in a quiet space where you can concentrate and consider the identities you have adopted in your life. An easy way to do this is to think about the different roles you play in your life. Identify what you seek to gain through using the identity you have chosen to focus on, and how you would feel if what you identify with was taken away.

2. Allow yourself to feel the emotional response associated with this situation. You may feel pain in your heart or stomach area. Some people have blocked their pain for so long that they don't feel anything. If this is the case for you, shift your awareness to your heart or stomach

area — whichever you think is best — and lift the lid off your pain. Then allow yourself to drop into the pain so you can feel it.

3. Don't get caught up in the story of the situation that caused the pain. Just picture or feel this pain as a black ball, and surround it with the light of your life force. The life force creates a sacred space within you where only truth is told.

4. Place your awareness in the black ball of pain and ask your body what belief you hold to have caused this use of identity, and when that belief was formed.

5. Be very still and wait for the answer to form in your consciousness. It sounds different than the normal chatter of your mind. It is profound and to the point. While you may "hear" what the belief you hold is, sometimes you may also "see" a picture of a person or an event linked to the formation of the negative belief. Accompanying this may be a reenactment of how the negative belief was formed that offers a wider perspective of that experience. Allow whatever you hear or see to play out, as though you are listening to the radio or watching TV. You find your belief was formed either when you were young or during a traumatic event.

6. If a person appeared in relation to the formation of your negative belief, ask them why they acted the way they did. In the light of your life force, their answer is honest and direct. You may ask clarifying questions, but keep the dialogue short and direct. The purpose is to get to the heart of the matter without obscuring it with unnecessary talk and questions.

7. Usually, this person says they are sorry for the way they acted. Even if they do not, it is necessary to exercise compassion and understanding in order for you to heal. Tell them that you forgive them, and do so from the heart. It is more powerful if you say it out loud. You may also choose to thank them for any positive things that they have contributed to your life.

8. If a person or an event does not appear, ask your body what is required to heal the negative belief. Wait for an answer to form in your consciousness. Sometimes it is necessary to simply forgive ourselves for

holding the negative belief, and putting ourselves through a series of traumatic experiences. Once again, it is more powerful if we forgive ourselves from the heart, out loud.

9. Burn through your ball of pain with the light of your life force. Then extend your light into every cell of your body to remove the negative belief.

10. Return your awareness to your heart or stomach area. Ask your body what positive belief you can hold to bring happiness into your life. Your body responds with a positive belief based on inclusion, deservedness, and abundance. Allow it to form in your consciousness. Once again, it is profound and to the point.

11. Cradle this positive belief and wrap the light of your life force around it. Then extend the light of your life force into every cell in your body to embed this positive belief. You may experience a series of positive realizations through this process. Enjoy them — they are a lovely part of the healing process.

For example, you may be a rescuer, which gives you a sense of purpose and belonging. You feel that the only way for you to be included is to save others, otherwise you don't deserve love and support. Hold the pain associated with this experience in a black ball and surround it with the light of your life force. Place your awareness on the black ball of pain. Ask your body what belief you hold to cause this use of identity, and when that belief was formed. You may discover you believe that you do not deserve to have a healthy, mutually supportive relationship, or to be appreciated for yourself outside of your role as rescuer. This belief may have formed in childhood, for example, when you cared for a grieving parent following a divorce.

In the dialogue with your parent, they may explain why they broke down and became overly-dependent on you following their divorce. They recognize that this was not an appropriate role for a child and ask for your forgiveness. Forgive them and yourself if you have repeated this rescuer role to your own detriment throughout your life. Burn through your ball of pain with the light of your life force. Then extend your light into every cell of your body to remove the negative belief. Ask your body what positive belief you can hold. The response may be: *I have happy, healthy relationships*, or *I am loved for who I am.* State your new, positive belief in the present tense to demonstrate that you are included and deserving, and that it flows to you through the abundance of the universe. Use the light of your life force to embed this belief into the cells of your body, and you are healed.

Once you change the beliefs which underpin your use of identity, it falls away. You no longer feel the need to use it to feel good about yourself. New situations flow into your life based on your new beliefs. For the best results, repeat the healing exercise for all of the identities that you use.

The irony is that we use identity to feel whole, but in doing so, actually perpetuate separateness. We deny ourselves the chance to be whole by being one with the universe. When you heal the use of identities, you realize you belong with everyone and everything. You reconnect with the universe and, in doing so, anchor yourself in a very powerful way. This creates enormous inner peace.

We are not the roles we play in life — mother, brother, lawyer, princess, or failure. Each of these definitions is too binding for our magnificence.

We are. That's it. Period.

Healing Relationships

Our relationships are the one aspect of our lives where the impact of our negative beliefs is most evident, and can cause the most unhappiness. Healing our personal relationships plays an important role in supporting our well-being by increasing how loved, happy, and safe we feel.

The most significant relationship for you to heal is that with yourself, so it is important for you to apply the exercises to yourself first. There is no point hoping that you will meet the perfect partner, or blaming your partner for everything that is wrong in your relationship, if you have not first taken steps to heal your own pain and negative beliefs.

The more pain that each person holds inside, the more likely it is that the relationship fails or is destructive. As we discussed earlier, people with large amounts of pain often project their pain onto other people. They also tend to sabotage relationships. If they are in a relationship with a person who has less pain, it is quite common for the person with less pain to walk away.

When both people hold large amounts of pain inside, cycles of emotional and/or physical abuse may be established to the detriment of both people. You can see why it's important to heal your pain and negative beliefs. Doing so takes the fuel out of the fire, enabling you to manage the differences that inevitably arise in relationships more calmly and rationally.

The beliefs of each person also interact with those of their relationship partner. This is true for both positive and negative beliefs. When you both believe that you are loved and accepted for who you are, you nurture each other. Conversely, when you both hold negative beliefs, the interaction of those beliefs can cause the relationship to falter.

For example, John was neglected by his parents as a child, and developed the belief that he does not deserve to be loved. As an adult, he began to view his wife Marilyn through his pain in the same way as he had his parents, and exhibited child-like behaviors which reinforced his belief that he was unloved — John avoided coming home, and refused to see Marilyn's point of view or take responsibility for his actions. Marilyn started treating John like a child in response to him acting like one. This was a further manifestation of John's negative belief.

Marilyn's parents had expected their children to be high achievers. She grew up believing that she could never be good enough and was not accepted for who she was. John's absences from home were a manifestation of her negative belief of not being accepted by those close to her.

You may be able to think of instances in your own life where your negative beliefs interacted destructively with someone else's.

John and Marilyn both judge themselves and blame the other for the failure of their relationship. In separateness, we are quick to judge ourselves and others for our perceived mistakes and shortcomings. We often fail to appreciate and build on the good things inside ourselves and in others. We stay fixed in recriminations based on past behavior, which only reinforces our negative beliefs as well as any fractures in our relationships. Judging ourselves and others creates both inner and outer conflict, and closes the path to healing our relationships[1].

Although we all hold negative beliefs, it doesn't mean that every relationship we have is doomed to failure. However, relationships are more likely to be healthy and successful when you both have taken steps to heal your pain and negative beliefs, and have positive attitudes towards yourselves and love.

People heal at different rates and at different times. Some people, even with large amounts of pain inside, feel so loved and supported by their partner that they are willing to address their pain and negative beliefs. Others need to be triggered by a life event before they take action. If you are ready to address your own pain and negative beliefs and your partner is not, that is okay. In the end, you are responsible for your actions and their impact on the world, and your attitude may inspire your partner to heal their own pain and negative beliefs.

In situations where both parties in a relationship simultaneously want to improve it, both need to consider and heal the beliefs that have contributed to the creation of tension in the relationship. Approaching the relationship from a perspective of inclusion, deservedness, and abundance involves seeing the spark of divinity in each other. Appreciating the other person and building upon the best in them and in yourself enhances the relationship and the well-being of you both.

You can both recognize when old patterns of behavior are occurring and consciously choose to focus on creating peace and love in your relationship by healing. Through healing, the amount of love and acceptance in the relationship grows. Both parties radiate their own inner peace and inner strength. They respect each other and are safe in the relationship. They nurture each other, encourage each other to shine, and be the best they can be.

Large waves of love, peace, and happiness ripple out from people in successful relationships, and positively impact those around them. Being in a happy and loving relationship is a lovely way to contribute to increased harmony in the world.

Healing Ourselves

Over time, you can turn your life around by making a concentrated effort to heal using the exercises. Of course, once you have mastered them, you do not have to do them in the order I have presented. You can choose the most appropriate one for the situation you wish to deal with.

When doing the exercises, if you find that you are beating yourself up for everything that has gone wrong in your life, take some time to identify the negative belief you hold and heal it. We all hold negative beliefs, and we are all responsible for their impact on our lives, and consequently, the world. The important thing is to recognize this impact on your well-being, happiness, and relationships. Accept the responsibility for holding the negative beliefs and your subsequent actions, and take steps to heal.

Sometimes the effects of healing are evident the moment that healing takes place. Other times, we only become aware when we look back after a period of time and realize that we are handling situations differently and attracting different people into our lives. Improvements to your inner peace, happiness, and overall well-being may happen incrementally. That's okay. Life is a journey. The way to measure our success is to feel happier and more peaceful within ourselves, and that our lives are continually improving.

By healing the negative beliefs underpinning your use of power and identity, and increasing your inner peace and sense of belonging, you are creating ripples of happiness that spread out from you into the world. You are improving your own life and touching those around you in positive and loving ways. And by participating in personal healing, no matter what role you play in life — truck driver or president — you are taking responsibility for your part in the world and making an important contribution to improving world harmony. Well done!

✍ Key Messages ❧

- Negative beliefs underpin our use of power and identity.
- Healing the negative beliefs which cause us to use power and identity creates inner peace, strength, and a greater sense of belonging and connection to others.
- When both people in a relationship heal their pain and negative beliefs, they shine and project love, peace, and happiness into the world.

COLLECTIVE HEALING

It's easy to see that, as we each project our increased inner peace and happiness into our spheres of influence, what a significant ripple effect this will have across the world. Together, we are already starting to make a difference. By not having to focus on pain and problems in our lives, we free up the attention required to address the world issues that concern us all. The next step in our healing journey is to address the beliefs we all hold that contribute to unhappiness in the world.

Ideas that are held to be true by a group of people are called *collective beliefs*. Collective beliefs have a greater impact in the world than individual beliefs, because their power is magnified by the number of people holding them. Groups of people of any size hold collective beliefs including nations, businesses, governments, non-governmental organizations, and pressure groups.

On a global scale, the manifestations of negative collective beliefs include war, the exploitation of others, and environmental degradation. These issues affect every country on earth. Their presence on this worldwide scale is evidence that we all hold the negative collective beliefs which cause them. This means that the responsibility of healing the negative collective beliefs that shape the world falls on all of us — not just world leaders, but also you and me. The relationship between our individual and our collective beliefs is shown in Figure 2.

Figure 2:
Our peaceful planet is created by healing our negative individual and collective beliefs.

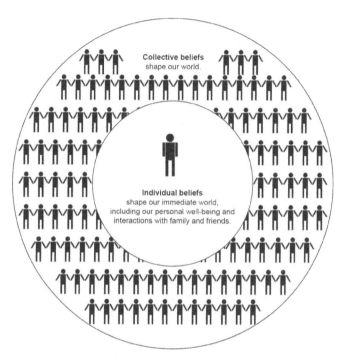

Collective beliefs
shape our world.

Individual beliefs
shape our immediate world,
including our personal well-being and
interactions with family and friends.

Positive collective beliefs are equally as powerful as negative ones. By healing our negative collective beliefs and replacing them with positive ones, we can bring about massive positive global change. The more of us that participate in healing our negative collective beliefs, the greater the positive global change will be. Our new way of perceiving ourselves, others, and our planet — through inclusion, deservedness, and abundance — provides us with a powerful basis to make the necessary changes to existing governance, industrial, and economic structures and bring about increased harmony and well-being around the world.

In the previous chapter, we discussed the mistaken use of power and identity to feel good about ourselves. The impact of both is nowhere more evident than on the world stage. While there are many negative collective beliefs based on separateness, undeservedness, and lack, in this chapter, we are going to focus on healing our most destructive collective belief. This key belief underpins the use of power and group identity at the international level, and our dominance over the earth.

The Use of Power and Group Identity

We have already considered the prevailing belief that to win and be strong is good. The human race has perpetuated this belief by creating mythology about the glory of battle and the righteousness of domination over others. The use of power manifests in the pursuit of wealth, war, and the exploitation of others through poverty, corruption, societal repression of women, drug trafficking, people trafficking, child slavery, and illegal prostitution.

People whose sense of self is strongly linked with winning and having power are willing to undertake incredibly destructive actions without thought to the impact on others. Sadly, there are no shortage of examples. Think of those who actively participate in war or corporate and financial manipulations to increase their personal power. Think of dictators and their cronies who vigorously repress dissent and amass fortunes while the people they rule starve. Think of those who participate in child prostitution — whether as pimps or as customers. These people undertake these activities repeatedly to feel good about themselves, because in reality the use of power is independent of personal well-being.

The impacts of the use of power are too great for us to continue to accept them as "just the way things are." The use of power perpetuates inequality and unhappiness, which in turn perpetuates the perceived need to fight. The result is that the well-being of millions of people living in war zones and in poverty is compromised.

Although there have been attempts to abate war and the exploitation of others, efforts have failed because the use of power is essentially what international relations is currently based on. Countries try to increase their power by buying more weapons, or by threatening others to get what they want. Other countries stay silent or condone violent actions when they shouldn't, for fear of upsetting a more powerful ally.

The use of power is even evident in what may be perceived as more peaceful activities such as trade, where countries negotiate to gain the upper hand for their citizens — even if it means that other people in the world must struggle to survive because they do not receive a fair price for their goods. You can see that by participating in these actions, we are holding ourselves separate from other groups of people. We are demonstrating our beliefs that some of us are more deserving than others, and there are not enough good things to go around.

It is easy for those who use power to justify their actions when they see others doing the same. Drug propagation and trafficking becomes justifiable when people cannot make a decent living legitimately due to the high level of corruption in their country. Similarly, a dictator can compare his hold on power with that of the permanent members of the United Nations Security Council, who refuse to give up their positions even though they reflect the global power distribution of 1945 rather than that of today.[1] To create lasting peace and increased well-being in the world, all of us need to heal the key negative collective belief underpinning the use of power.

Let's look now at the use of group identity. The use of group identity has created more destruction and strife in the world than anything else by perpetuating separateness between groups. In order to feel as though we belong, we find a very small amount of common ground and then exclude any other people who don't share the same small bit of common ground.

The use of group identity is very much tied with the use of power on the international stage since groups use identities to gain or retain power. Common group identities include religion, ethnicity, nationality, and left and right wing ideologies. Think of any war — the wars in Iraq, Bosnia and Kosovo, Africa, the World Wars, even terrorism. They are all rooted in both group identity and power.

The use of group identity creates great polarization when one group believes their ideas or way of life is always right and another is always wrong. This leads to actions that we justify in our separateness, which otherwise we would neither consider nor condone. When we believe that our group deserves something and another doesn't, or that our ideology is right and another isn't, we convince ourselves that it doesn't matter if the other group is killed, forced from their homes, or exploited; this is what they deserve. This is how we justify creating and stockpiling weapons capable of devastating, inhumane effects.

We adopt group identities because they provide us with a sense of belonging, and a collective power to try to get our own way. However, in adopting these group identities, we separate ourselves from others and fail to appreciate our common humanity. When we, as a group or nation, exercise power over others, all we are doing is perpetuating the negative collective belief that this is the only way in which humankind can relate to each other — in a struggle of separateness to win and feel good about ourselves.

This restricts us from connecting with others in ways which provide benefits for everyone involved. There are a myriad of other ways humans can interact to better meet the needs of us all. And the reality is, and always has been, that we are all one — one with everyone and everything on earth, and with the rest of the universe. So when we try to exercise power over others, all we are doing is subjugating or destroying ourselves. It doesn't seem such a desirable outcome anymore, does it?

Dominance over the Earth

We also fight on an international scale over resources. The use of power and group identity is inextricably tied up in these wars, as well. We justify these conflicts by convincing ourselves that there isn't enough to go around, and that one group deserves more access to a resource than another group does. The "War over Water," a series of confrontations between Israel and its Arab neighbors over the use of water in the Jordan River system in the mid-1960s, is an example of this.[2]

Control over the flow of resources to a conquering group increases their power. This was particularly evident during the period of colonialism from the late fifteenth to the twentieth centuries. Over the course of this time, the flow of human and natural resources from Asia, the Middle East, the Caribbean, South America, and Africa boosted the wealth and power of European nations and created, then nurtured, the United States of America. Some argue that it was also evident in the most recent Iraq war, which provided western countries easier access to Iraq's great oil reserves.

Once again, we see the principles of separateness, undeservedness, and lack at play in these conflicts. We hold ourselves separate from other groups of people, believing some are more deserving of resources than others, and focus on a lack of resources. If we approach these situations from the perspective of inclusion, deservedness, and abundance instead, then we recognize that everyone deserves equal access to resources, and we develop ways to ensure that everyone has access to resources without depleting them. We are one, and when we deny one group access to resources, we are also denying ourselves.

Not only do we fight one another over resources, we also fight the earth itself. We have embraced the idea that the earth is separate from us and exists for us to exploit and destroy as we please. The impacts of our actions are evident throughout the world. Think of the mining operations across the world that function without adequate environmental controls. They pollute the earth while in operation and long afterwards because no one is willing to pay the cost of cleaning them up.[3]

Think also of the Aral Sea in Central Asia, the volume of which has shrunk by approximately 85 percent due to the diversion of water for agricultural irrigation. This shrinkage has caused ecosystem collapse, fisheries loss, and soil salinity.[4] In addition, approximately 24,000 species of plants and animals in the world are known to be threatened with extinction because of unsustainable human population growth, pollution, poaching, and habitat destruction.[5]

Our dominance over the earth is based on separateness, undeservedness, and lack. The reality is that we are totally reliant on the earth for our survival. Our use of power over the earth blinds us to ways in which resources can be used to increase the well-being of everyone without further damaging the earth.

Healing Our Most Destructive Negative Collective Belief

The use of power and group identity, and our dominance over the earth is underpinned by one key negative collective belief — we have to struggle to survive. We believe that by accumulating and using power, we guarantee our survival. Similarly, the more of us that stick together in a group, the more likely we are to survive. And the more we use the earth's resources, the better off we are. We hold ourselves separate from others and the earth, as though some of us are more deserving than others, and there is not enough to go around.

By now you are familiar with the exercise to heal negative beliefs. We are going to use the same exercise to heal this negative collective belief, but this time, the positive collective beliefs that you embed at Step 10 are articulated for you. Remember, the healing of this negative collective belief is everyone's responsibility because we all hold it. By going through the exercise below, and embedding the positive collective beliefs which form the basis of our peaceful planet, you are contributing to positive change on a global scale.

Once again, you get the best outcome when you are very honest with yourself. Don't judge or beat yourself up. Just allow what comes up to come up, and follow the steps to heal it:

1. Sit in a quiet space where you are unlikely to be distracted, and think about the belief that we have to struggle to survive.

2. Allow yourself to feel the emotional response associated with this belief. You may feel pain in your heart or stomach area. Once again, if you don't feel anything, shift your awareness to your heart or stomach area — whichever you think is best — and imagine lifting the lid off your pain. Then allow yourself to drop into the pain so that you can feel it.

3. Picture or feel this pain as a black ball, and surround it with the light of your life force. The life force creates a sacred space within you where only truth is told.

4. Place your awareness in the black ball of pain, and ask your body when this belief was formed.

5. Be very still and wait for the answer to form in your consciousness. It sounds different than the normal chatter of your mind. It is profound and to the point. While you may "hear" what the belief you hold is in your mind, sometimes you may also "see" a picture of a person or an event linked to the formation of the negative belief. Accompanying this may be a reenactment of how the negative belief was formed that offers a wider perspective of that experience. Allow whatever you hear or see to play out, as though you are listening to the radio or watching TV.

6. If a person appeared in relation to the formation of this negative belief, ask them why they acted the way they did. In the light of your life force,

their answer is honest and direct. You may ask clarifying questions, but keep the dialogue short and direct. The purpose is to get to the heart of the matter without obscuring it with unnecessary talk and questions.

7. Usually, this person says they are sorry for the way they acted. Even if they do not, it is necessary to exercise compassion and understanding in order for you to heal. Tell them that you forgive them, and do so from the heart. It is more powerful if you say it out loud. You may also choose to thank them for any positive things that they have contributed to your life.

8. If a person or an event does not appear, ask your body what is required to heal the negative belief. Wait for an answer to form in your consciousness. Sometimes it is necessary to simply forgive ourselves for holding the negative belief, and putting ourselves through a series of traumatic experiences. Once again, it is more powerful if we forgive ourselves from the heart, out loud.

9. Burn through your ball of pain with the light of your life force. Then extend your light into every cell of your body to remove the negative belief.

10. Return your awareness to your heart or stomach area, and focus on the following two positive collective beliefs: *power is to have inner peace and spread that peace throughout the world*, and *we are one with each other and the earth*.

11. Cradle these positive beliefs and wrap the light of your life force around them. Then extend the light of your life force into every cell in your body to embed these positive beliefs. You may experience a series of positive realizations through this process. Enjoy them — they are a lovely part of the healing process.

Some of you may find that this key negative collective belief is linked to a personal experience, while others may go back in time to when the belief was first formed in human history. Both healing experiences are equally valid and effective. Feeling greater inner peace and a sense of belonging and connection to others and the earth is a key result of this exercise. This is because when we release the struggle for survival, we create the space for what we need to flow to us. The truth is that we never needed to struggle to gain, as we can create what we want through the abundance of the universe. This creates inner peace because our survival is guaranteed.

When we relinquish the separateness of identities, we feel a greater connection with others. We realize that we are all equal and all deserving of having our needs met. We realize that we are not our ethnic group, or our country, or our religion. We are far more than all of these combined. We are.

This shift in our collective beliefs results in the desire to increase harmony and improve the well-being of all people around the world, whether they are our neighbors, our enemies, or those living in a far-off land. The incalculable result of acting on this desire is that we magnify our own happiness and well-being. When we are giving of ourselves, and connected to each other through inclusion, the loving energy flows right back through us.

We also better appreciate how we are one with the earth, and reliant on its well-being for our survival. We value our exchange of both material and energy with the earth through biodegradation and photosynthesis. Our bodies are at least 60 percent water by weight, and half the air we breathe remains in our lungs while some of the remainder circulates in our bloodstream.[6] We recognize that by looking after the planet, we are also taking greater care of ourselves.

All the attention and energy we devoted to maintaining power and group identity, can now be used to develop creative solutions to world problems, working together because we all belong, and we all deserve love, acceptance, and respect. We value each other and our planet and create new ways to support ourselves while minimizing the damage to the earth. We take greater care in rehabilitating the damage we have done, thereby increasing the well-being of all life forms across the planet.

Reconciling Opposing Groups

Once we have started to build some momentum in healing this key negative collective belief, we can begin in earnest to heal situations at the local, national, and international levels. We all have a role to play in this healing by acting in whatever capacity we can, and providing support to those who seek to implement positive change.

Healing with the greatest impact is done by the leaders of groups, whether they are presidents, rebel leaders, non-governmental organizations, CEOs, or industry representatives. Taking steps to heal the situation at hand for the well-being of the people they represent, and the earth, demonstrates true leadership. This involves undertaking discussions with opposing groups to resolve differences.

We discussed earlier that whatever we hold inside of us, be it pain or peace, is what we project into the world. For this reason, it is important for leaders to take steps to heal the pain in their own hearts prior to entering discussions. Remember the new definition of power — *to have inner peace and to spread that peace throughout the world.* Those who have peace in their hearts are more likely to enter discussions with the right intent and open minds. They can construct creative solutions, and accept the changes necessary to create peace and rehabilitate the environment in their part of the world.

There are additional factors to be considered when reconciling opposing groups of people. Groups of people of any size hold collective beliefs in addition to the key belief that we have to struggle to survive. For example, one group may believe that the opposing side doesn't deserve to exist, while the opposing group may carry a victim identity. A company may believe that it deserves sole access to a resource because it paid for it, while traditional owners may believe that those companies only ruin the land.

Some negative collective beliefs and group identities have been carried over generations. In situations where there is a long-running fracture between groups, there is a greater tendency to stay fixed in recriminations based on past behavior, particularly where reconciliatory processes have failed. This behavior only reinforces our negative beliefs and further fractures the relationship. This is a deliberate choice stemming from beliefs strongly rooted in separateness, undeservedness, and lack, played out through the use of power and group identity. For this reason, each party are, as a group, to heal the key belief that we have to struggle to survive, and any other negative collective beliefs about themselves and the other parties, before entering negotiations.

By addressing these beliefs first, each party becomes aware of how their negative collective beliefs contributed to the creation of the situation. The realizations experienced through the healings help the group gain a broader understanding of the situation and to fully forgive. By forgiving themselves and others, and replacing those beliefs with positive ones based on inclusion, deservedness, and abundance, the group can start to envision the kind of peaceful and plentiful life they, and their soon-to-be former adversaries, deserve.

Once this process is complete, opposing groups can meet to end their differences. Spending time healing negative collective beliefs helps all players to see our commonality and the life force in all of us. From this place, creative solutions which address inequality, and enhance the well-being of all parties and the environment can be found. Wonderful things can happen by harnessing the energy of a group and using it for good.

✺ Key Messages ✺

- The more of us that participate in healing the key negative collective belief underpinning the use of power, group identity, and our dominance over the earth, the greater positive global change will be.
- Our peaceful planet is based on the following positive collective beliefs:
  o Power is to have inner peace and spread that peace throughout the world.
  o We are one with each other and the earth.
- All the attention we devoted to maintaining power and group identity can now be used to develop creative solutions for global issues, working together because we all belong and all deserve love, acceptance, and respect.

Up Next

The following chapters outline the steps we can take to create greater harmony, equality, and well-being for all life forms on the earth. Together, they form a blueprint for the future based on inclusion, deservedness, and abundance. We will explore creating lasting peace in areas of conflict around the world, living in harmony with the environment, and modifying the way our economy is structured to better support us and the earth.

PART 2

HEALING
THE WORLD

CREATING PEACE IN
POST-CONFLICT SOCIETIES

A s you know, at any given point in time, armed conflicts are being fought in a number of places around the world. One of the reasons that war has been so pervasive is because it creates wealth and influence for the small number of individuals in power. As we discussed in the previous chapter, they use power and group identity to perpetuate separateness, undeservedness, and lack.

For the majority of people, armed conflict has a massively negative impact. People lose their homes and members of their family. They experience torture, and are traumatized by the violence and their forcible displacement. Most people welcome the end of war, grateful for a chance to live their lives peacefully. In recognition of this, since the end of the Cold War, greater efforts have been made at an international level to resolve conflicts through peacekeeping deployments and the facilitation of peace talks.

Frequently though, attempts at creating peace in post-conflict societies fail. Warring parties revert to fighting again, a dictator takes power, countries remain impoverished, and particular groups are marginalized. This is because:

- until now, reconciliation between warring parties has not included the healing of negative beliefs, and
- reconciliation is just the first step in creating long-term peace and improving the quality of life for the millions of people living in areas of conflict.

Lasting peace and stability can only be achieved when people live in societies which are structured to enable harmonious, meaningful, and equitable participation, and in which their needs are met. These societies are based on the principles of inclusion, deservedness, and abundance. There have been many attempts at creating this in post-conflict societies, but most have fallen short because the negative collective beliefs of those affected by war have not been healed, and new governance structures have not been properly implemented.

The rebuilding of a region or nation devastated by war requires sustained intention and effort. During this time, all of the following activities are required to develop a fully-functioning, peaceful society:

- healing the negative collective beliefs of those affected by war
- introducing democracy effectively
- creating the structures required to sustain peace
- creating a free economy and
- creating an active civil society.

Let's explore the impact of old behaviors based on negative beliefs, and what can be done based on positive collective beliefs to build peaceful societies. By fully implementing the actions outlined in this chapter, we can turn conflict zones into regions of inclusion, deservedness, and abundance, and spread peace and stability throughout the world.

Healing the Negative Collective Beliefs of Those Affected by War

Even after peace has been brokered, people may still hold onto discriminatory, negative collective beliefs towards their former adversaries. This undermines the prospects for long-term peace particularly in areas where former rivals cohabitate. Peace is fragile in its early stages, and relapses into violence are common. Positive messaging campaigns to modify people's attitudes are vital for at least the first five to ten years of peace. These inclusive messages are designed to build acceptance of each other and project how the nation or region can perceive itself. These messages are based on the positive collective beliefs that power is to have inner peace and spread that peace, and that we are one.

For example, positive messaging about multiculturalism over an extended period of time in Australia has resulted in widespread acceptance of immigrants and a multicultural society. This messaging, coupled with an active citizenship program, reinforces the positive contribution immigrants make to the nation, and that we are all Australian despite our different ethnicities.[1]

Similar messaging in post-conflict societies can focus on creating a new nation together where all groups belong regardless of their religion or ethnicity. Targeted campaigns and dedicated healing workshops for ex-militants can be held in areas where tensions are high to diffuse a potential return to violence *before* it happens and help them reorient their lives. In this way, the potential to fall into old behaviors is recognized and managed by consciously focusing on healing and creating peace.

Healing negative collective beliefs helps facilitate reconciliation efforts like truth and justice commissions, and the repatriation of land. It provides a positive basis for admission of guilt, forgiveness, and the acceptance of others, which is crucial to the success of these efforts. Healing and positive messaging campaigns create the space for everyone to focus on creating a stronger and cohesive nation, and on living and working side by side in peace and freedom.

Introducing Democracy Effectively

Much effort has gone into introducing democracy around the world in the last fifteen to twenty years. While democracy is not perfect, it is the only truly inclusive system of governance in which citizens can actively and equitably participate. Their participation in public debate allows for alternative solutions to be developed for a nation's issues. Democratic governments are accountable to the people. They create and operate within laws which are uniform, predictable, transparent, and which apply to everyone — providing the greatest level of personal freedom with the lowest risk of abuse of power.[2] Unfortunately, full democracy has failed to take hold in a number of countries for three main reasons.

The first is that general knowledge about democracy and how it works is poor. Some leaders in post-conflict societies have maintained their use of power based on separateness, undeservedness, and lack, and have not adapted from ruling systems which concentrate power in the hands of a few. Those leaders who have committed war crimes, participated in non-democratic governments, or amassed fortunes during war or by stealing public funds, are good examples of this. For a peaceful society to fully develop, it is best if these leaders are not permitted to stand for election.

Sustained education campaigns for other existing and would-be politicians in post-conflict societies are required so that they can actively learn via example. This can be done through long-term mentoring programs that bring together ethical, experienced, successful former leaders and politicians of democratic nations, with interim and newly elected leaders and politicians in the post-conflict nation. The education program teaches politicians how to govern in a democratic system, and reinforces the fundamental principle that the elected serve the people. It includes decision making for the long-term benefit of the country, rather than seeking short-term gains within an electoral cycle — something that politicians from other, stable nations can also benefit from learning.

The general public of a newly democratic nation also may not necessarily understand how democracy works, or their rights and responsibilities within a democratic system. Education and messaging campaigns are required to help them understand the pillars of democracy, and their role in it. This education program can extend beyond elections to governance, the role of the military, the judiciary, and civil society, and freedom of the press. It includes what behavior they can expect from democratic leaders and what behavior is unacceptable.

Educating the public in this way ensures that people can participate meaningfully in their new democratic system, and reinforces the positive collective beliefs that power is to have inner peace and spread that peace, and that we are one. Increasing their understanding, coupled with inclusive messaging campaigns, decreases public tolerance of corrupt, self-serving leaders and war criminals.

Once people understand the benefits of democracy, they are more likely to choose leaders who, with peace in their hearts, use their position to make sure the needs of the citizens are met. The use of consistent messaging about creating a democratic nation builds support and momentum for the changes that are required to develop democratic structures and a functioning economy over the long term. Messaging can also be used to inspire people to work together to realize a common vision for the future.

The second reason that democracy has failed to take hold in post-conflict societies is that forming political parties and holding elections are insufficient to sustain peace when they are not founded on a solid, inclusive basis. The way parties are formed, how election campaigns are carried out, and when the elections are held, are all important.

For example, political parties formed on religious, ethnic, or tribal lines are never going to create a unified society, because their very existence focuses on separateness between groups of citizens. Similarly, practices like the inequitable distribution and harassment of voters unfairly influence the outcome of elections, serving the interests of elites whose beliefs are based on separateness, undeservedness, and lack. These practices result in a disenfranchised group within the population whose interests are not represented, and who may resort to violence in order to be heard.[3] Elections held without positive messaging, adequate mentoring of politicians, education of the public, and before democratic institutions have commenced, are likely to lead to poorly implemented democracy with non-accountable and non-transparent governments.[4]

The following ground rules for creating truly inclusive democracies can be established and adhered to from the outset:

- The form of government chosen is that which provides the greatest freedoms and best represents the citizens in that region.
- There is a clear separation of religion from state. The leader of each political party is to be democratically chosen either by the party or the people, without influence from religious leaders.

- Political parties cannot be formed or campaign on the basis of religion, ethnicity, or tribe. Parties whose platforms contain policies which are discriminatory or repressive towards groups of people are banned.
- The law-making body of government, often known as Parliament or Congress, is structured so that power cannot be concentrated in the hands of the president or the elite.
- The first election is held between five months and one year post-ceasefire, to allow adequate time for messaging, training, and for work to commence on establishing democratic institutions. An interim government can be established in the meantime.
- Citizens may vote for anyone they freely choose in procedurally fair elections, and their free choice is respected.
- The functioning of government is in accordance with the country's constitution, and any changes to the constitution is done through public referendum.
- New laws require a majority consensus in all houses of Parliament or Congress.

The third main reason why democracy frequently fails in post-conflict societies is that too much attention is paid to forming political parties and holding elections, at the expense of creating and sustaining the actual institutions which are the backbone of democracy. A fully functioning democracy has:

- a law-making body, often known as Parliament or Congress, and a public or civil service
- a judiciary, which interprets and applies the law and
- military and police forces, which protect the country and enforce the law.

Each is constrained by laws which provide checks against the misuse of power in any one institution. These laws are respected and upheld to maintain stability and peace.[5] Together they create a balanced system of governance, and equal attention to creating all three institutions in post-conflict societies is required.

Creating the Structures Required to Sustain Peace

Parliament and Public Administration

Creating a new parliament and public administration, including all the rules and procedures of law making, tax collection, and expenditure on public goods, requires a great deal of work. We have already discussed the need for education of politicians in post-conflict societies. The provision of aid funded, outside expertise is required over a sustained period to work with new parliamentarians and public servants. This helps them to understand their jobs, establish the best fit of laws and procedures in the local context to justly carry out the functions of governing, and ensure probity in the expenditure of public funds.[6] Democratic countries can set up and fund dedicated teams of people with the requisite skills and experience to build the capacity of governments in post-conflict societies around the world.

For the public administration to be impartial and transparent, senior public servants are to be appointed by a public service commission based on merit, rather than by politicians. This way, senior public servants can be trusted by citizens for their integrity, impartiality, and expertise in delivering government funded policies and programs. Allowing the impartiality of the different branches of government is an active demonstration by politicians of the positive collective belief that power is to have inner peace and spread that peace throughout their country.

Judiciary

Many judicial systems in existence are based on separateness and undeservedness, and do not provide equal application of the law to all. Factors such as gender and social class influence both the laws and judgments in these systems, perpetuating inequality. In a democracy, laws are created by parliament and are applied equally to everyone through the judiciary, demonstrating inclusion.[7] Some aspects of the judiciary in post-conflict societies may be based on traditional systems, so long as they are free from corruption, follow nationally accepted procedures in open hearings, and apply consistent and fair judgments to all citizens regardless of gender, ethnicity, and social standing.

The judiciary is to be independent from parliament in order to operate as an effective check against the power of parliament. Once again, the appointment of judges, including high court judges, is to be done on merit through a public service commission rather than through political affiliation. This way, judges are promoted on the basis of their ability to do their job well, and their judgments are more likely to be impartial and uninfluenced by those in power.

Similarly, the budget of the judiciary, which is often decided by parliament in countries transitioning to peace, is to be sufficient to allow the judiciary to undertake its duties until such time as it can fund itself through court fees. An insufficient budget leads to a backup of cases to be heard, greater corruption, and a loss of faith in the legal system. Once again, the provision of aid funded, outside expertise is required over a sustained period to work with local experts to establish procedures that ensure the effective functioning of the courts, and that everyone is given a fair trial.

Military and Police Forces

In most conflicts, the military and police have been used against ordinary people to promote the interests of a small group of people in power. The size of the military in particular is disproportionate to the general population, and military coups overthrowing fragile democracies in the early post-war years are common.[8] The use of power and group identity is particularly evident in these cases. External expertise is required to transform the military, in both size and function.

The first step in transforming the forces post-conflict is to develop laws and policies which reflect the role of the military and police forces in a peaceful country. The military is then downsized and restructured to meet the aims of these new laws and policies. The amount of weaponry is correspondingly reduced, and military and police officers are retrained in their new roles, with an emphasis on understanding their role in a peaceful and inclusive society.[9]

This last point is crucial. Sanctioned, unethical conduct such as genocide, rape, and torture by military and police personnel are manifestations of the use of power and group identity, which require healing in military and police personnel. Similarly, ordinary people who have been terrorized by security forces distrust them, and need to heal their negative beliefs about them. For this reason, the new role of security forces are to be included in the education campaign for the general public of a newly democratic nation.

Creating a Free Economy

The other aspect of governance that creates stability in a country is a free and functioning economy. Those who are gainfully employed in activities that improve their standard of living are less likely to return to violence out of boredom or perceived injustice. Having meaningful work and contributing to building a peaceful nation reinforces the positive collective beliefs that power is to have inner peace and spread that peace, and that we are one. Economic recovery can be stimulated by the creation of infrastructure and public services, and by undertaking economic reforms to encourage business development and foreign investment.

Rebuilding infrastructure to replace what has been lost though war — roads, houses, schools, hospitals, universities, airports — and introducing new industries and technology, provides jobs and skills development for men who may have been in the military, rebel groups, or displaced by war.[10] Having this infrastructure and technology in place provides greater opportunities to compete globally in other economic activities including trade.[11]

Unfortunately, the provision of aid funding for activities such as the rebuilding of infrastructure in post-conflict and poorly developed societies has in the past been for the short-term only, much less than initially committed by donor countries, and subject to much corruption. Analysis of the use of aid in the countries at the bottom of the development scale found that approximately 11 percent of financial aid leaks into the military budget, resulting in 40 percent of the military budget being financed by aid.[12]

Corruption is, of course, not limited to these countries. It has been built into the functioning of a great number of economies around the world, both those at peace and at war. Created by negative beliefs based on separateness, undeservedness, and lack, and played out through systems of alliance rather than merit, corruption generates great inequality and has no place in an inclusive democracy.

Research has shown that money provided early in the reform of societies retards good governance, so aid is to be provided at this stage in the form of expertise instead.[13] The reformation of institutions, downsizing of the military, and training of politicians, bureaucrats, and security force personnel through foreign expertise early in the post-conflict era provides time for new beliefs and systems to be established. Peacekeepers can be used during this period to provide security force expertise and training, and to start rebuilding the region.

Anti-corruption messages are an important part of the education and messaging campaigns for politicians, bureaucrats, the judiciary, and the general public. Through these messages, new beliefs of equality, honesty, and hard work replace corruption, and create a culture of trust, innovation, and entrepreneurship.[14] Once this has taken place, the state can provide good governance and transparency guarantees to donors before financial aid is provided to build infrastructure. Donors can help by committing to providing aid through expertise and funds for up to ten years, as it realistically takes a nation this long to rebuild after war.

To promote inclusion, deservedness, and abundance, infrastructure is to be provided equally across the nation or region. This ensures that all citizens receive equal access and therefore have equal opportunity to participate in economic growth. This is an important component of creating a peaceful and inclusive society. The provision of public services such as schools and hospitals for all people to access and mix in, regardless of their gender, ethnicity, or level of wealth, reinforces the positive collective belief that we are one and everyone is treated equally. Participation in education provides disadvantaged groups the means to improve their quality of life, and the skills base for economic growth.

The introduction of a common language for education and interaction with government institutions also creates inclusion.[15] This does not preclude the teaching of other languages in school or at home, but serves rather to break down ethnic barriers. Many people in the world are multilingual, being taught mostly in one language but provided with training in others.

Long-term economic recovery is also stimulated by creating a free and functioning economy through laws and government policies. Post-conflict governments can do this by undertaking internal reforms that encourage entrepreneurial culture while ensuring social and environmental protection. These reforms include:

- having sufficient regulation to ensure that business, including the finance sector, is accountable to society, while enabling flexibility in business operation
- privatizing some state owned assets in an honest and transparent process, while keeping others for the benefit of the nation
- keeping inflation low
- limiting government borrowing
- developing labor laws to prevent exploitation and
- developing environmental laws to limit the impacts of pollution.

The confidence of international financial markets can be regained by implementing these measures, encouraging healthy foreign investment, and debt can be paid through trade surpluses.[16]

Creating an Active Civil Society

Of course, governments are not the only actors in post-conflict societies. Ordinary citizens form business, social, and philanthropic groups in what is known as *civil society*. Civil society forms the social fabric of a nation, and is essential for effective democratic government and a well-functioning economy.[17] With the spread of the internet, civil society is playing an increasingly large role in informing public debate, problem solving, and building support for good causes nationally and internationally. Civil society holds governments and corporations accountable to the people, and introduces new, progressive ideas into society.[18] It enables equitable and meaningful participation in society based on the positive collective belief that we are one.

Civil society tends to disintegrate during conflict. International non-governmental organizations play an important role in recreating civil society in post-conflict societies, as they provide aid, rehabilitation, and training to local groups until they can function on their own. These organizations improve conditions on the ground, and help to create social cohesion. They are also instrumental in introducing new concepts into post-conflict societies, such as gender equality and environmental protection and rehabilitation.

An important part of a strong civil society is the presence of free press. Conflicts frequently occur in regions where the media is not free to report the activities of government, businesses, or people. In these situations, the media is heavily controlled and censored by the state and independent media outlets are forcibly shut down.

Using power and identity, governments use state controlled media to relay carefully crafted messages that glorify the government and repress the people. They do not tell citizens about their activities which serve the elite or harm those who speak out against the government. The use of the media in this way demonstrates negative beliefs based on separateness, undeservedness, and lack, and allows governments to avoid scrutiny and accountability. Worse, the media can be used to perpetuate division and fuel unrest by relaying racial messages, as occurred in Nazi Germany during the Second World War and the Rwandan genocide in 1994.[19]

Freedom of speech is an important element of democracy. It provides for the expression of opinions and encourages debate. Linked to this concept is freedom of the press — that is, that media outlets can accurately report on the activities of government, businesses, and citizens without interference or censorship. The press plays an important role in ensuring that the government is accountable to the people it serves by reporting on the government's progress towards its stated goals, such as the implementation of democratic institutions and a free economy. The best way to ensure that a range of opinions and viewpoints are heard is to legislate that the media is not monopolized by one or two companies, or the government, actively demonstrating that power is to have inner peace and spread that peace.[20]

Any restrictions on the freedom of the press are also to be legislated. These laws can include the banning of hate speech and praise of violence, prevention of libel and slander, and respecting the privacy of citizens. Government material and decisions can be classified according to the level of security, and become publicly available after a period of time in line with their security classification.

All unclassified, government documents are to be available under freedom of information legislation to ensure transparency and accountability.

You can see from all of the actions outlined in this chapter that building lasting peace in post-conflict societies requires sustained effort and intention. The great thing is that everyone can contribute. We can all create international pressure for opposing parties to reconcile by joining the social debate, and lobbying politicians to help create peace. People in donor countries can contribute aid funding through their taxes, and through donations to non-governmental organizations. Those with the appropriate expertise can work in post-conflict zones alongside local citizens to create peaceful and equitable societies. Citizens can contribute by healing their negative collective beliefs, participating in civil society, and using their individual skills and talents to rebuild their country. By working together, we can create lasting peace in post-conflict societies, and spread that peace throughout the world.

Key Messages

- Creating peace in post-conflict societies involves messaging and actions which consistently reinforce that power is to have inner peace and spread that peace throughout the world, and that we are one.
- It requires sustained intention and effort to build fully-functioning, peaceful societies. Everyone has a role from governments and non-governmental organizations, to everyday citizens.
- By fully implementing these actions in post-conflict societies, we can turn conflict zones into regions of inclusion, deservedness, and abundance, and spread peace and stability throughout the world.

CREATING LASTING
PEACE WORLDWIDE

There are many places around the world which are not at war, but where people are subject to suffering and hardship. These situations, caused by inequitable governance, the accumulation of weaponry, and the exploitation of people, are all based on separateness, undeservedness, and lack, often played out through the use of power and identity. In this chapter, we discover how to heal these manifestations of repression and destruction.

None of these have been seriously addressed on a worldwide scale before. As we heal our negative beliefs, we recognize that we are one, and that each of us deserves to live our lives in abundance, regardless of who we are and where we come from. From this basis, we are moved to create greater harmony and equality, and improve the wellbeing of all people across the world, so that we all live in peace and freedom.

Spreading Democracy

In the previous chapter, we spoke about the importance of introducing democracy effectively into post-conflict societies. There are many countries in the world that are not democracies or fully-functioning democracies, whose citizens are denied the opportunity to actively and equitably participate in their system of governance. In absolute monarchies, single-party states, religious regimes, and military dictatorships, public dissent of the rule of those in power is systematically and often brutally repressed.

Nations where democracy has not been fully implemented are characterized by the following features:

- rule by elites
- poor governance
- banning of opposing political parties by those in power
- ethnic politics resulting in polarization of the community and paralyzed decision making in parliament
- systemic repression of and violence against part of the population based on religion, gender, or ethnicity
- resources and revenues exploited and distributed through cronyism and nepotism, with little benefit flowing down to local communities
- contradictory legislation and regulations that make it difficult to conduct business
- corruption in the government and the judiciary
- limited accountability by the military leading to human rights abuses
- limited public scrutiny of government actions, with press freedom limited by legal and regulatory restrictions, reporters subject to violence and intimidation, and pressure placed on media outlets by governing elites
- elections marked by polarizing politics, campaign violence, and fraud, resulting in low voter turnout
- incumbents using state resources to aid their re-election, or using family members as proxies to get around term limits
- vote buying, intimidation, and mobilization of ethnic groups to support specific candidates and
- a non-transparent electoral commission.[1]

What is common in all these examples is the use of power and identity to create gains for a small number of people, while ordinary citizens cannot participate in their society in a meaningful and equitable way. An ordinary citizen may be unable to:

- run for parliament
- freely express their opinion
- know the truth about how they are being governed and how their taxes are being spent
- live in peace without suspicion of others
- vote for who they want
- bid for and win government funded contracts or
- honestly create wealth.

The many demonstrations for democracy in Iran, Tunisia, Egypt, Libya, and Syria demonstrate that people want to participate in a more inclusive, fair, and transparent system of governance. This is true no matter where they live, or what their religious or ethnic background is. It is the responsibility of the rulers of non- and partially democratic nations to listen to their citizens, heal the negative beliefs which underpin their use of power and identity, and transition to full democracy. These actions demonstrate that power is to have inner peace, and spread that peace throughout the world.

The transition of many Eastern European nations from communism to democracy in the 1990s demonstrates that it is possible for this shift to occur peacefully, particularly when transitioning nations reach out for help and advice. Democratic nations can influence transitions to democracy by applying international pressure, providing expertise in aid reform, and by stipulating conditions for becoming members of influential international groups.

Healing the use of power and identity, and spreading fully-functioning democracy throughout the world addresses other global issues. It reduces terrorism and rebellion. People who feel that they are treated equally and can peacefully have a say in the running of the country, whether through voting or direct representation to politicians, generally don't feel the need to resort to violence to be heard.[2] It also reduces the arms trade, because we have removed the need to fight, and introduced democratic mechanisms to resolve differences. Spreading democracy is therefore a critically important part of creating sustainable peace throughout the world.

Reducing Weaponry

Weapons are manifestations of our key negative collective belief that we have to struggle to survive. They are what we use in our fights to win and feel strong, and have been used for centuries to perpetuate separateness, undeservedness, and lack. It seems that in recent times, as the wealth in the world has increased and technology has advanced, we have allowed our perceived struggle for survival to overwhelm us and have lost control.

The full extent of what we have created may shock you. In 2015, the military expenditure of the world's governments was an estimated $1.7 trillion.[3] The numbers of nuclear, chemical, and conventional weapons stockpiled are similarly frightening. There are an estimated 15,000 nuclear weapons, 4,100 of which are operational, and enough fissile material in the world to make tens of thousands more warheads.[4] There are approximately 10,000 metric tons of chemical warfare agents, more than 875 million small arms, millions of missiles, and billions of cluster bombs and other munitions.[5]

By increasing peace in the world through the healing of our key negative collective belief, we eliminate the need to spend the same amount of money on defense, and to keep the massive amount of weaponry that we have accumulated. In truth, we didn't need it in the first place, as many of the weapons created have never been used. The effects of some weapons are potentially so horrible and so far reaching that sane people have avoided their use, and resolved situations diplomatically.

As we no longer need them, these weapons, as well as the other machinery of war including tanks, submarines, aircraft, and remote weapons systems, can be decommissioned and destroyed. Materials can be recycled where possible, and hazardous materials treated and safely disposed of. Remaining stockpiles of weapons are only to be enough for minimal, non-provocative defense. In an increasingly peaceful and interdependent world, the use of healing and discussion to resolve problems with mutually beneficial solutions, will become the norm.[6]

We can redirect the money we have been spending on weaponry to activities which improve the well-being of all life forms on earth. For example, we can use it to help nations transition to democracy, and to rehabilitate damaged land and waterways across the world, including those polluted by nuclear and chemical military waste. We can use it to improve health services and education in developed countries, and to provide health services, education, and food security in developing countries. We can also use the money to support environmentally sustainable economic development, protect tropical forests, and help improve the resilience of countries experiencing the impacts of climate change.

In addition to these measures, we can provide the greatest security for future generations by completely dismantling the industry which has the most potential to badly damage our planet — the nuclear industry, which creates both nuclear weapons and generates electricity. The generation of electricity using nuclear energy was developed as a way to justify the continued manufacture of nuclear weapons following the bombing of Hiroshima in World War II, and remains heavily subsidized by governments.[7] The two facets of the industry are intrinsically linked, and both have the capacity to negatively impact humans and the environment in ruinous ways.

Nuclear weapons are the most devastating that man has developed, capable of widespread destruction. A single nuclear bomb can destroy entire cities, kill millions of people, cause cancer and long-term genetic damage in those who survive, and contaminate air, land, and water for miles around the original blast site for thousands of years.[8]

Participants at the 2013 Oslo Conference on the Humanitarian Impact of Nuclear Weapons, including official delegations from 127 nations, determined that no country or international body such as the United Nations can adequately address the immediate humanitarian emergency caused by a *single* nuclear weapon detonation. They also agreed that nuclear weapons have devastating long-term effects, and that these effects will not be constrained by national borders. They will impact nations and people both regionally and globally.[9]

While there are practices in place that limit the leakage of nuclear material and technology originally designated for electricity generation into weapons production, the spread of nuclear weapons to "non-approved" countries including India, Pakistan, Iran, and North Korea through electricity programs demonstrates that the two cannot ever effectively be disassociated.[10]

There are a number of other reasons why the discontinuation of nuclear energy is a good idea. Firstly, it makes economic sense to do so. The most advanced nuclear reactors built by Japan in 1996 produce electricity at double the cost of a natural gas power plant and 33 percent more than a high capacity wind plant. $120 billion has been invested worldwide in nuclear technology over the last thirty years, with little progress in lowering the costs or risks.[11]

Secondly, we have learned the hard way that accidents at nuclear reactors happen, and that we simply do not know how to adequately deal with these accidents or their long-term effects. The crisis at the Fukushima Daiichi nuclear power plant, resulting from the earthquake and subsequent tsunami in Japan on March 11, 2011, is the most recent example. Nuclear material was released into the atmosphere and contaminated water into the Pacific Ocean, causing mass evacuations, international concern, and an overnight decline in Japan's seafood industry.[12]

The incident has been classified by Japan's Nuclear and Industrial Safety Agency to be as serious as the reactor meltdown at Chernobyl in 1986, where two million people still live on contaminated ground.[13] With radioactive material leaking into the Pacific Ocean over four years, it remains to be seen how all the contaminated material at Fukushima will be managed, and what the long-term social and environmental impacts of the disaster will be. The full decommissioning process is expected to take at least three decades.[14]

Finally, there are long-term environmental concerns about nuclear waste which have not been adequately addressed. Nuclear waste from electricity and weapon production stays radioactive for thousands of years, and we do not know whether the containers in which they are stored will last even two hundred years.[15] That leaves a lot of radioactive material that will be released into the environment at some point in time, causing radioactive poisoning, cancer, and genetic mutation.[16] Given the gravity of the impact of nuclear weapons and the environmental damage caused by the release of nuclear material, we can best ensure the well-being of the planet by destroying nuclear weapons, decommissioning power plants as soon as possible, and switching to renewable energy sources.

The arms and nuclear energy industries create employment for a great number of people around the world. Once weapons stockpiles have been reduced, and nuclear power plants decommissioned and destroyed, these people can be retrained in industries which promote harmony and well-being, such as environmental rehabilitation and the development of environmentally friendly technology.[17] Reducing weapons and redirecting the funds and energy towards activities which support life demonstrates our positive collective beliefs that power is to have inner peace and spread that peace throughout the world, and that we are one with each other and the earth.

Ending the Exploitation of People

The exploitation of people is another manifestation of our key negative collective belief that we have to struggle to survive, played out through the use of power and identity. Corruption, human trafficking and slavery, and drug production and trafficking are all actions based on our separateness from others, whom we believe deserve to be exploited so that we can gain riches. These actions lock people in cycles of abuse and poverty, denying them the opportunity to live freely, in abundance.

Corruption

In the previous chapter, we noted that corruption has been built into the functioning of a number of economies around the world, and relies on systems of alliance rather than merit or equality. The problem is more widespread than you may realize. The 2015 Corruption Perceptions Index developed by Transparency International shows that serious public sector corruption is perceived to exist in 68 percent of the 168 countries in the index.[18]

Corruption in government involves the misuse of public funds, including aid, for private gain. It may manifest in a number of ways including:

- the awarding of large government contracts to friends and family in non- transparent tendering processes

- public services being provided in areas with ethnic ties to the ruling elite
- vote buying
- government officials demanding bribes for undertaking their normal duties, such as providing law and order, "free" school education, or certificates so that people can conduct business, or buy and sell property
- judges and law enforcement personnel accepting bribes from criminals and
- the theft of public funds by government administrators at every level, including into the private overseas bank accounts of ruling elites.

It is no surprise then that corruption undermines democracy and the rule of law. Citizens become reluctant to pay their taxes when they see their money disappear, or benefit select groups of people, while the majority continue to live in poverty. Institutions that are intended to provide checks and balances within the system often lack the resources and independence from the government to function properly, coming under pressure to curb investigations.[19] People's faith in their government is destroyed, and injustice is fueled, leading to conflict. Those who complain about this injustice generally do not have access to civil and political rights because democracy is either not present or is not fully implemented in their country.[20]

In countries with natural resources such as timber, diamonds, and oil, economic activity is often restricted to their exploitation and retarded in all other sectors. These countries rely heavily on the revenues gained from these resources, and funds are frequently diverted into the hands of the ruling elites rather than to the benefit of the population at large, leaving people in poverty.[21]

Corruption is a cause of poverty and a barrier to overcoming it. Those countries at the bottom of the Corruption Perceptions Index tend to have the highest rates of malnutrition, as people have to pay more for scarce resources.[22] Corruption retards economic development. Business people who wish to conduct or grow business are retarded by the payment of regular bribes to officials, or by a lack of funds to bribe politicians to amend regulations to make conducting business easier. Because citizens struggle to survive in societies where corruption is present, they copy the actions of their governments and participate in corruption too, demanding additional payment for services provided in the local economy.

The presence of corruption therefore becomes a deterrent to investment. People with capital in a corrupt country choose to invest overseas, and international investors similarly place their money elsewhere.[23] The situation is so bad that the amount of legally and illegally gained money flowing out of the developing world into overseas bank accounts is more than all the money flowing in the opposite direction in the form of loans, aid, or payment for exports.[24]

Human Trafficking and Slavery

We tend to think of human trafficking and slavery as something that happened in colonial times, but it continues today. It is estimated that 21 million victims globally are forced to work against their will with no pay in domestic servitude, agricultural work, garment manufacture, the fishing industry, construction, and sex work.[25] Approximately 66 percent were trafficked across national borders, while the remainder were trafficked within their country of origin.[26]

If you think it doesn't happen where you live, think again. Between 2010 and 2012, victims of 152 nationalities were detected in 124 different countries.[27] Approximately 70 percent of all victims are women and girls and 33 percent are minors.[28] 53 percent of victims are trafficked into sexual exploitation, and 40 percent are trafficked into forced labour.[29]

Drug Trafficking

Drug trafficking and use impacts every level of society — from global security and national governance, to individuals, families, and local communities. With an estimated $600 billion in profits in 2010, drug trafficking has become the main source of income for organized crime, terrorists, and insurgents.[30] The drug trade increases the level of violence and corruption in source and transit countries, particularly in Latin America, the Caribbean, and West Africa. In some countries, the drug trade involves senior political figures, while in others drug traffickers have become powerful enough to take on the state through violent confrontation.[31]

The human impact of the drug trade is huge in both source and receiving countries. An estimated 120,000 people have died since 2007 in Mexico's War on Drugs, a war between the Mexican government and local drug cartels, for example. Another 27,000 people are missing.[32] Approximately 250 million people used drugs in 2014, with 29 million of these being drug dependent.[33] The negative impact of drug use on individuals, families, and communities is well-documented. As with any addiction, people use drugs to block the pain caused by negative beliefs, such as not being deserving of love and acceptance. Healing of these negative beliefs is required for a person to release their dependence on drugs.

Both human trafficking and drug production and trafficking occur predominately in underdeveloped parts of the world, where poverty and corruption are prevalent. People turn to these crimes due to the inability to earn an income from legitimate sources. For example, only one quarter of all farmers involved in illicit drug crop production have access to the knowledge and resources to help them move into alternate industries.[34]

These scary statistics demonstrate the extent of the exploitation of others. The good news is there are a number of steps we can take to increase the well-being of affected people around the world.

The first step is to heal our personal and negative collective beliefs, and to undertake positive messaging campaigns which reinforce our positive collective belief that we are one. This messaging reminds us of the equality of all people, thereby modifying people's attitudes and making exploitative practices both unwanted and unnecessary. Targeted campaigns to heal ruling elites, government officials, trafficking suppliers, and customers can also be implemented.

The second step is to spread fully-functioning democracy. It is difficult to hide corruption and slavery in a system that promotes equality.

The third step is to build economies to eradicate poverty and give people alternate, legitimate means of supporting themselves.

Finally, we can further develop crime prevention capabilities and foster the rule of law to eradicate corruption and human and drug trafficking. By implementing all of these steps over a sustained period of time, we can end the exploitation of people.

Global Governance

It has probably occurred to you that the social and political issues we have discussed so far, together with the environmental and economic issues that we will discuss next, cross international borders and therefore require us to work together at the global level to fully heal them. The only structure we have at the international level, the United Nations, is not currently being fully utilized to undertake this kind of collective problem solving. This is because countries participate in the United Nations only as it serves their best interests, rather than considering the best interests of the planet as a whole. The use of power and group identity is strongly at play here.

A clear example of the use of power is the way the United Nations Security Council is structured. This body is responsible for international peace and security, and its permanent membership is restricted to the five countries that developed nuclear weapons prior to 1965 — China, France, Russia (formerly the USSR), the United Kingdom, and the United States. Its capacity to be effective, for most of its existence, has been limited as the two main players, the then USSR and the United States, were divided against each other in what became known as the Cold War. During that time, both countries built up significant nuclear arsenal and brought the world closer to World War III than we were comfortable with. Essentially they did not provide international peace and security at all.

More than twenty years after the end of the Cold War, the Security Council remains ineffective, as nations responsible for selling weapons into areas of conflict veto measures to create peace in those regions. In 2012, both Russia and China *three times* vetoed any action to be taken against Syria, whose ruling dictator was waging a war against Syrian citizens who wanted a democratic government.[35] Their reluctance to act has created the space for terrorist organizations to thrive.[36] While it is recognized that the membership of the Security Council should change to better reflect the power distribution across the world today, consensus cannot be reached as to which countries should join the current five to become permanent members. There is no discussion of any of those five relinquishing their seats.

The Security Council can only truly fulfill its mandate of ensuring international peace and security when it is comprised of members who have demonstrated their commitment to peace and improving the well-being of people and the planet, rather than those who have the most destructive weapons. In our peaceful planet, in recognition of the relationship between security and environmental destruction, the mandate of the Security Council can include the consideration of environmental matters as well as peace. Members can be responsible for providing leadership and direction in healing social, political, and environmental issues, thereby facilitating the move to greater harmony, equality, and well-being. They can represent our new definition of power — they have inner peace, and spread that peace throughout the world.

To be eligible for election onto the Security Council, nations can meet a number of criteria, including being a fully-functioning democracy which upholds human rights, and being committed to looking after the environment. If members fail to meet these criteria at any point in their term, they automatically lose their positions. Elections can be held every five years. Members of the United Nations can remain bound to accept and carry out the decisions of the Security Council.[37]

Such a structure can provide international leadership on solving the collective issues that face the planet. With healing occurring across the globe, the space and impetus required for nations to work together to further improve the well-being of us all are available in this structure. The rest of the United Nations system can be reconfigured and resourced to help nations carry out the work required to solve these issues.

The Role of the Media

We cannot discuss healing on a global level without mentioning the impact of the media. The media plays an important role by informing the public about what is occurring in the world around us, and by shaping public opinion. Demonstrating separateness, undeservedness, and lack, the focus of the media is mostly on what is wrong with the world, based on the belief that "only bad news sells." Media reporting is also frequently incomplete, inaccurate, and sensationalized, so we do not receive an accurate or balanced portrayal of what has occurred.

The media can support global healing by reporting in an accurate and balanced way on all matters, allowing for a range of opinions to be expressed.

They can also play a significant role in promoting global harmony by reporting on the progress of people and nations meeting peace and environmental objectives. They can feature more stories about how people have helped each other and interacted in ways which bring about greater understanding.

With this approach, our achievements are promoted and celebrated, and receive as much air time and space in the newspaper as those situations that require healing. The media can therefore help create momentum for even more healing, and advance the well-being of people and the environment across the world.

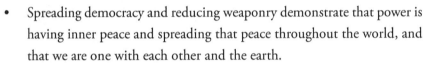

⟳ Key Messages ⟲

- Spreading democracy and reducing weaponry demonstrate that power is having inner peace and spreading that peace throughout the world, and that we are one with each other and the earth.
- Ending the exploitation of people demonstrates that we are one, and improves the well-being of millions around the world.
- Restructuring the United Nations is vital to effectively build and sustain peace, and human and environmental well-being around the world.

Up Next

We are not the only living beings on the planet. We are part of a beautiful web of natural existence on which we are dependent for our survival. To date, our impact on that web has been disproportionately negative. Next, we turn to healing the environmental damage caused by our key negative collective belief, to enhance the well-being of all living things on the planet.

RETHINKING RESOURCE USE

The natural world in an untouched state is a complex interconnected web of living and inanimate systems in dynamic balance. As in all interconnected systems, impacting on the balance in one area of the natural world has consequences in other areas. We humans have always taken resources from the natural world to sustain ourselves, but in our separateness from the earth have failed to appreciate the growing impact of our consumption on those systems. We have interfered with them so much that it has become apparent the earth no longer has the capacity to support the way we produce and consume.[1]

In Chapter 3, we healed our separateness from and dominance over the earth, and realized instead that we and the earth are one. With this shift, our world view becomes ecocentric, rather than human-centric. We now place ourselves in the ecological system, rather than sitting above it, and consider our impact on the environment in every action we take. With an ecocentric world view, we can work together to create new ways to support ourselves while minimizing the damage to the earth. The first things we will consider from our new world view are those that have the greatest impact on the environment — our dependence on non-renewable sources of energy and our rates of consumption.

Sustainable Energy Use

Around the world, those of us who have access to electricity and cars rely predominately on coal and oil to power our economies and lifestyles. Both, unfortunately, are the most polluting forms of energy that we can use, and because we use them in abundance, we pollute in abundance. An estimated 120 million tons of the pollution that causes climate change are released into the atmosphere every day — a figure that continues to increase.[2]

In recent years, greater attention has been paid to the causes and impacts of climate change. When I studied environmental engineering in the early 1990s, climate change was discussed as something that would probably happen in fifty years' time. Twenty-five years later, climate change is front and center of environmental, and increasingly, mainstream discussions, because our use of oil and coal has grown exponentially in that time.[3]

The burning of coal and oil is the primary cause of climate change, as it releases carbon dioxide into the atmosphere in greater volumes than the earth can process. This causes unnatural variations in the climate — for example, low rainfall and extended drought in warm parts of the world, increased cyclone and bushfire activity, and increased ambient temperatures causing glaciers to shrink and reducing the formation of ice in arctic regions. Increased water in the oceans through the addition of melting glaciers, as well as through thermal expansion, causes sea levels to rise, threatening the existence of people and ecologies in island nations and other low-lying parts of the world. The acidity of the ocean has also increased due to climate change.[4] Everyone in the world has directly experienced at least one of these impacts in recent years.

Scientists working in this field agree that the climate changes we are currently experiencing have been caused by man, rather than being natural variations to weather patterns over time. The governments of the world formally endorsed this view in the Cancun Agreements formulated at the 2010 United Nations Climate Change Conference.[5]

What are the impacts of climate change?

We stand to lose a number of plant and animal species due to rising temperatures, both in low-lying areas, which will be flooded, and in alpine and arctic areas where species are used to colder temperatures. We are already experiencing a decline in threatened alpine species, and damage to internationally significant coral reef systems because of climate change.[6] Once lost, those ecosystems cannot be regained.

The 600 million people who live in low-lying areas, such as islands and river deltas, stand to lose their homes as the sea level rises.[7] People in Bangladesh, Vietnam, and Mozambique have already been displaced following intense flooding in recent years. Drought in grain-producing countries led to food shortages around the world between 2006 and 2012, and people living in drought affected areas are expected to continue experiencing low rainfall, affecting their ability to grow food.[8] People who rely on glaciers as their primary water source are already experiencing water scarcity, and may not have enough water to sustain their communities into the future. People's homes will continue to be destroyed in bushfires, floods, and cyclones.[9] Those affected migrate as a result, placing a strain on resources and undermining stability in other regions.[10]

The Intergovernmental Panel on Climate Change stated in their Fourth and Fifth Assessment Reports on Climate Change that unmitigated climate change would be likely to exceed the capacity of natural, managed, and human systems to adapt in the long term.[11] Scientists are now saying that the climate is changing faster than they originally projected, with greater extremes of temperature. They also say that the small commitments that world governments have taken to date to address climate change, most of which are unmet, are not enough to mitigate against serious temperature rises.[12]

The impacts of climate change impose an emotional and financial cost, the brunt of which is expected to be borne by developing nations, who can least afford it.[13] Yet climate change is caused primarily by those of us in developed and rapidly industrializing nations. In an inclusive world, we recognize that this is no longer an appropriate burden to place on them. We also recognize that vulnerable ecosystems, no matter where they are, are something we want to protect for future generations to enjoy.

The use of oil also has other security, social, and environmental impacts. The huge global demand for oil has resulted in large flows of money to ruling elites in a number of countries. The United States, the largest consumer of oil in the world, spends approximately $900 million a day on foreign oil, with about 47 percent of this money going to elites in countries with poor governance regimes.[14]

Some elites in oil rich countries purchase weapons and provide support to terrorist organizations with oil money. Because they have this large income stream independent from any revenue raised from taxes, they are not strongly answerable to their citizens, and are also somewhat immune to international pressure. Democracy is stymied, people are repressed, and the lack of environmental legislation means that oil extraction and production pollutes local environments that citizens depend on for their survival.[15]

The good news is that there is quite a lot we can do to address climate change, and embed our positive collective belief that we are one with each other and the earth. All it requires is for us to start taking action now.

The first thing we can do is to become more energy efficient. In our age of consumerism, many of us have shifted to larger homes with more gadgets and bigger cars, without considering the impact on the environment. Few homes, for example, are built to be energy efficient through passive solar design or the adoption of other energy efficiency measures, requiring more electricity for heating and cooling. In these larger homes, we have more lighting and more TVs, which use more electricity. Similarly, some of us are buying large cars with low fuel-efficiency, requiring the use of more fuel and creating more pollution.[16]

Adopting more energy efficient measures does not affect the way we work or live, and has an enormous impact on the amount of energy we use. It is estimated that the adoption of energy efficient measures in buildings across the United States alone will result in a 23 percent reduction in energy consumption, saving $1.2 trillion for an investment of $530 billion.[17] It is always cheaper and faster for a society to conserve energy where it is being used, than it is to build more power plants. Energy efficiency therefore makes both good economic and environmental sense, and can be implemented through improved building, vehicle, and appliance energy efficiency standards.

The second thing we can do to mitigate climate change is improve existing power plants with newly available technology. Traditional power generation is actually incredibly inefficient and produces almost three quarters of all carbon dioxide emissions. In the United States, it is estimated that electricity rates can be cut by 40 percent and carbon dioxide emissions by half just by upgrading power plants and transmission systems.[18] Similarly, coal-fired power stations in China and India have been built using old technology without the equipment to reduce their environmental impacts.[19] Upgrading power plants and transmission systems will make a huge difference in reducing the amount of pollution produced.

The third thing we can do is to take serious steps to move to the wholesale use of renewable energies. Some people believe that using natural gas as an energy source also addresses carbon change. While natural gas contains less carbon than coal and oil, it still releases carbon dioxide into the atmosphere when it is burned. Using natural gas instead of coal and oil only slows the rate of climate change; it does not genuinely address it. According to a report by Lord Nicholas Stern and think-tank Carbon Tracker, between 65–80 percent of listed reserves of coal, gas, and oil will have to remain unused if we are to meet the internationally agreed targets to avoid the point at which global warming is expected to irreparably harm civilization and our environment.[20]

Only a wholesale move to renewable energy will address climate change in the long run. This involves greater adoption of both distributed power systems and large-scale production of renewable energy, with a view to phase out carbon-based electricity altogether.

In distributed power systems, individual consumers create electricity in their homes or businesses using a range of renewable energy sources, such as solar panels or small wind generators, and sell any excess power back into regional power grids. This reduces the need to build additional large-scale power plants in developed countries, and is a particularly attractive option in developing countries that cannot afford huge power plants. It is an inclusive solution, in which everybody contributes to electricity generation. It has been estimated that wide-scale adoption of distributed energy systems will reduce the cost of transitioning to a low carbon future by as much as $144 billion by 2050.[21] Saving that much money is certainly worth serious consideration.

Adopting both distributed power systems and large-scale production of renewable energy will also reduce the water used in electricity generation by an estimated 75 percent.[22] This is significant in dry countries such as Australia where the water can be used for agricultural production, or diverted back into the environment to improve the health of waterways.

Until recently, the renewable energy sector has suffered from a severe lack of funding and support, and wind farms and solar plants only existed in a few forward-thinking places around the world, such as California, Denmark, Germany, and Spain.[23] Huge amounts of government funding for research and development, as well as subsidies and tax incentives, have been directed solely at the nuclear, oil, and coal industries over many years. In 2014, fossil fuel subsidies were $493 billion, creating an uneven playing field for the development of renewable energy.[24]

Despite the impact of fossil fuel subsidies, some progress has been made. Major investments by China and the United States in recent years have contributed significantly to growth in the renewable energy sector. Renewable energy accounted for 19.2 percent of total global energy consumption in 2014.[25] With increased demand and funding for clean energy, we can expect to see further improvements and cost reductions in the technology, in the same way we've seen with mobile phones and computers.

We can also establish intercontinental electricity grids, with electricity generated in windy and warm places transported through high-capacity, high-efficiency transmission lines to nearby countries. The creation of these "super grids," coupled with the transition to fully-functioning democracies and the eradication of corruption, has the potential to contribute to economic prosperity and regional stability in the developing world. Electricity generated in Northern Africa and Central America from solar farms, for example, can be used domestically and transmitted to Europe and the United States, respectively.[26]

There are a number of other things that governments can do to direct change in the energy sector. Domestically, they can create legislation that drives the development of energy efficient buildings and subdivisions, fuel-efficient cars, and efficient power generation. A fuel tax can be used to deter the use of gas guzzling cars, and help fund research into the development of non-oil dependent vehicles.[27]

Tax incentives can also be used to upgrade existing power stations and transmission systems. To encourage innovation and the adoption of distributed power systems, governments can redirect the subsidies and tax incentives from the nuclear, coal, and oil industries to the renewable energy sector. The development of renewable technology provides exports for nations that are quick to adopt it, as Denmark, Germany, Japan, and China have already discovered.[28] Governments can also extend the area of protected forests, which remove carbon from the atmosphere, and require electricity companies to generate an increasing percentage of electricity from renewable sources.[29]

Internationally, governments can set meaningful binding targets and work together to systematically and transparently reduce greenhouse emissions. World governments are making some progress at United Nations Climate Change Conferences, but there is scope for greater emissions cuts, binding targets, and agreements on emissions accounting. The most promising initiative so far is the creation of a Green Climate Fund, which aims to provide $100 billion a year by 2020 in financial and technological support to help developing nations build their economies using renewable energy sources under sustainable development principles.[30]

The fund will also be used to protect tropical forests and help build resilience to the impacts of climate change. While this is a great initiative, thus far governments have been slow to commit money to the fund.[31] The money required is around only 6 percent of what we spend on weapons each year. In our peaceful and inclusive world, we can pay for this fund by redirecting the money previously used for weapons production. Alternatively, we can pay for it with the money raised through a tax on speculative currency transactions, an idea which is explored further in Chapter 10. By taking these ecocentric actions to address climate change, we can halt the production of carbon pollution, and protect vulnerable people and ecosystems.

From Consumerism to Sustainability

The amount of resources we consume also has a huge impact on the environment. This manifestation of our separateness from and dominance over the earth has increased exponentially in the last fifty years. World consumption of goods and services increased from $4.9 trillion in 1960 to $30.6 trillion in 2006.[32] That's a sixfold increase, but the human population only increased by a factor of 2.2 in the same period.[33] This means our consumption per person increased threefold per person in five decades. To feed our appetites for more things, metals production grew sixfold between 1950 and 2005, oil eightfold, and natural gas consumption fourteenfold.[34] Annually, 60 million tons of resources are extracted — 50 percent more than thirty years ago.[35] And our consumption continues to grow.

The impact of our consumption has resulted in the destruction of forests, species loss, declining soil fertility, polluted water supplies, climate change, and increased waste. The Ecological Footprint Indicator compares our human demand on nature with the earth's biocapacity — the amount of land and sea area available to supply key resources and ecosystem services like the production of oxygen. We now use the resources and services of 1.6 earths.[36] Obviously, we don't have 1.6 earths. We only have one, and if we continue to use it in the way we have been, the earth will not be able to sustain future generations.

Our key negative collective belief that we have to struggle to survive causes an emptiness that we try to fill with more and more things. We think that having more things will make us feel happy and secure. Indeed, the argument for increasing our consumption in the last 50 years is that our well-being has improved and we are happier. This is an erroneous link. Research has shown that subjective measures of well-being, such as the number of people who consider themselves very happy, have not increased since 1975.[37] Once our basic needs have been met, our personal well-being is independent of the number of things we have in our life.

Happiness comes from inside of us — from healing our negative individual and collective beliefs, and freeing ourselves — not from what we possess. We can create more meaning in our lives by helping others and helping to restore the earth, actively demonstrating that we are one with each other and the earth.

The most important thing we can do to reduce the impact of our consumption on the earth is consume less. We spend excessively and define ourselves by what we have to cover up how undeserving, unloved, insecure, and worthless we feel inside. When we heal our negative beliefs, we realize that we do not need enormous homes, lavish weddings, multiple cars, gadgets, handbags, or new clothes every season to make us look beautiful or demonstrate that we are the best. Our beauty and inner peace radiates from us instead. It is who we are and our positive impact on the world, not what we have, that is important.

Similarly, there is no need to buy an upgraded model of something if the one you have works fine. It's better for the environment if you use it until it is no longer functional, and then recycle it whenever possible, so that the materials can be reused in a new product. At the moment, we only recycle a small number of products — newspapers, cardboard, glass, cans, some plastics, and Styrofoam — and for the most part we do not recycle goods comprised of more than one material, like chairs.

Most of our waste goes into landfill, rather than being reused or recycled as a resource for new goods. We've established that we can't keep extracting new resources from the earth in the way that we have been. So we have to make greater use of the resources we have already extracted, rather than burying them. This involves a wholesale change in the way we manufacture products.

"Cradle-to-cradle" manufacturing is manufacturing from an ecocentric world view. It involves eliminating waste and pollution by recycling the components of old products into new products, and returning organic material to the soil, placing us in the ecological system. It models nature in balance, which is the most efficient system in existence.[38] Embracing this model of manufacturing, and building products which are designed to last, rather than break or go out of style after a short time, will have an enormous impact on our resource use. Governments can apply tariffs to virgin materials to encourage the use of recycled materials. The subsidies that are currently provided for the use of virgin materials can be redirected to businesses that recycle and use recycled materials in their products.[39]

The use of virgin resources impacts people as well as the environment. As with oil, most virgin resources come from the developing world, and provide large flows of money to ruling elites. Once again, this stymies democracy, and also keeps people trapped in poverty. Elites know they will receive huge profits from the sale of their country's natural resources, so they fail to diversify their country's income base by moving into other sectors, such as manufacturing and services.[40] This failure to diversify their economy leaves their population vulnerable to huge variations in natural resource prices, and unable to generate their own wealth. If you do not have a stake in the timber sold from tropical rainforests, for example, whatever you do for a living is not likely to generate much of an income.

We as consumers can be powerful drivers of the shift to sustainable goods, but first we need better information about the environmental and social footprint of the products we wish to purchase. There have been steps taken in tracing the origins of products and rating their sustainability, for example through GoodGuide, Walmart's sustainability index, and Sourcemap.[41] Some retailers like Ikea and Home Depot are committed to increasing their sales of products from sustainable sources.[42] However, this action has not been adopted by manufacturers and retailers across the board.

What we need is internationally standardized product labeling which rates the environmental and social footprint of each product. The rating can take into consideration:

- whether the product is manufactured with recycled or virgin resources
- where those resources came from
- where each component was manufactured
- the amount of pollution generated in the creation and transport of the product
- the amount of pollution use of the product will generate
- how long the product is expected to last
- whether the product is recyclable
- whether the people who manufactured the products were adults and were paid fair wages and
- the extent to which the manufacturer embraces environmental stewardship and social responsibility.

This concept extends to food labeling. The factors that can be taken into account include:

- where the ingredients were grown
- whether sustainable farming practices were used to produce each ingredient of the food product
- the extent to which synthetic pesticides and fertilizers were used
- whether natural habitats were destroyed or modified to create farms for the ingredients
- the amount of pollution generated in the creation and transport of the food product
- whether the people who grew and harvested the ingredients were adults and were paid fair wages and
- the extent to which the food company embraces environmental stewardship and social responsibility.

The rating can be displayed on the packaging of all products, with scanning of the barcode by a phone app revealing the full details from the international standards website. Using this system, through our spending power, we as consumers can knowledgably and deliberately choose products that are socially and environmentally responsible, thereby influencing manufacturers and retailers to adopt environmentally and socially responsible practices.

Any tendency for companies or consumers to be slow in adopting responsible practices can be overcome by legislating the application of this international labeling system for all products. Governments can also legislate against the import or development of the worst rated products, and impose tariffs on those that are poorly rated. Similarly, retailers can choose to only provide environmentally sustainable products for sale, and place pressure on suppliers to produce more sustainably.[43] These actions will shift consumer practices, and force product manufacturers to improve their environmental and social practices or risk going out of business.

Resource Use in the Developing World

78 percent of consumer purchases are made by 16 percent of the world's population living in the sixty-five highest income countries. Many in the developing world, particularly in China, aspire to first-world lifestyles.[44] Cars in particular have become a status symbol there. If the consumption rates of the Chinese rise to that of the First World, the rate of use of the earth's resources will double.[45] That means that we will be using the resources of 3.2 earths. We definitely don't have 3.2 earths.

That doesn't mean that the Chinese and others in the developing world cannot enjoy an increased standard of living. At the moment, a great deal of resource extraction occurs in developing countries and, as we discussed in the previous section, they receive very little direct benefit. We are all equal in our inclusive world, and deserve to participate in the abundance of the earth. We just need to be smarter about how we use the resources available to us, and how we preserve the earth for future generations. A rebalancing of our resource use around the world, along with an overall reduction, is required.

An increase in the standard of living in developing countries does not need to come at the expense of the environment. With the financial and technological support from already developed countries, developing countries can build their economies and improve their standards of living by embracing non-polluting, sustainable technologies. One way they can do this is to become more involved in the manufacture and exportation of products using recycled materials. Developing countries are already paid to accept garbage from other countries, from which they recover materials.[46] In separateness, currently a great deal of this work is done in the absence of environmental and labor laws. We can address this as we further inclusively develop this industry.

The reduction of consumption rates, and the reuse and recycling of resources, however, will not be enough to completely bring human demand in line with the earth's capacity to support us due to our rate of population growth. It is estimated that the world's population will grow from 7.5 billion people in 2016 to approximately 9.6 billion people by 2050.[47] Most of this growth is expected to occur in the developing world.

There are a range of reasons why large families are the norm in developing countries. In many of these countries, the children are expected to look after their parents when they grow old. With basic health services and a high infant mortality rate, parents have more children to ensure that some will survive to take care of them. Women tend not to be socially empowered in many of these countries as well. Many are not well-educated and do not have a say in the use of birth control, where it is available, or in how many children they will bear.

In an inclusive world, we recognize the equality of men and women. Everyone has the right to access health care and education, and the right to choose how many children they will have. Active healing of negative beliefs and positive messaging campaigns can be used to modify people's attitudes to the empowerment of women and the use of birth control.

Research has demonstrated that women who are educated are socially empowered to make their own decisions about the number of children they want.[48] We can extend education to all children regardless of gender in order to improve their well-being and reduce birth rates. We can also significantly address unsustainable population grown by providing health care facilities to improve child mortality rates and distributing birth control.

Aid can be used to establish dedicated health centers in developing nations around the globe. These centers can be a collaborative achievement between:

- the relevant governments of developing and developed nations
- local and international universities
- pharmaceutical companies
- the not-for-profit sector and
- the United Nations.

Health centers can be staffed by local and international experts who run the hospitals, clinics, and training centers. They can conduct research into local health issues such as child mortality and the prevention and treatment of diseases which significantly affect the working age population, including malaria, tuberculosis, and AIDS. Any intellectual property developed is to be transferable to other dedicated health centers. They can work with pharmaceutical companies to develop low cost drugs (where they do not already exist) to treat these diseases. The health centers can also train community health workers from each village. After their training, the health workers can return home and teach their neighbors about disease prevention, birth control, and safe birth practices. They can also dispense antimalarial and AIDS drugs, mosquito nets, and birth control.[49]

The extension of education and healthcare will substantially improve the well-being of people around the world while decreasing unsustainable population growth, reducing our impact on the earth, and demonstrating that we are one with each other and the earth. These measures, when combined with reducing and rebalancing resource use, ensure that everyone participates in the abundance of the earth while respecting its capacity to support us.

 Key Messages

- Using renewable energy and reducing our consumption demonstrates that we are one with each other and the earth.
- It is not what we have, but who we are and our positive impact in the world that is important.
- Reducing and rebalancing resource use, and decreasing population growth ensures that everyone participates in the abundance of the earth while respecting its capacity to support us.

FEEDING EVERYONE
SUSTAINABLY

We all have to eat, and the way the earth provides us with food is the clearest and most tangible expression of our reliance on it for our survival. Yet in our separateness from the earth, we have ignored the growing impact of our methods of food production on the environment. In our separateness from each other, we have inequitably distributed food around the world. Up to half of the world's food is thrown away while over 795 million people go hungry every day.[1]

In this chapter, we fully explore these manifestations of separateness, and discover how to heal them through the sustainable production of food and rehabilitation of the earth. By taking ecocentric actions, which recognize that everyone deserves to have enough to eat and that we can produce food in harmony with our environment, we can increase the well-being of all living things. We can also ensure that the earth can continue to support us into the future, demonstrating that we are one with each other and the earth.

Sustainable Agriculture

Most of us are aware that forests have been cut down to create farmland on a large scale around the world over the last twenty years. But you may not be aware of the extent of the damage. Subsistence and commercial farming together are responsible for a whopping 80 percent of global deforestation, which translates to the loss of an estimated seven million hectares of forest annually, just from agriculture[2]. Figures can become a bit meaningless, so imagine you are standing in the middle of a single crop, such as palm trees, stretching miles in every direction as far as the eye can see, where forest used to stand. Or imagine you are standing in hectares filled with grazing cattle, where the Amazon rainforest used to stand.

Forests play an important and complex role in the web of life. They regulate the climate, create oxygen for us to breathe, maintain soil stability, clean water by taking up nutrients, and provide homes for their inhabitants, both human and animal. By cutting down forests, we contribute to climate change, reduce rainfall in the affected area, increase soil erosion, decrease water quality, lose biodiversity, and drive species to extinction. In a world in which we and the earth are one, we recognize that we need forests to sustain us.

Scarily, only 13 percent of the world's forests lie in protected areas. The easiest thing we can do to address their loss is protect the remaining forests and their indigenous inhabitants by creating legislation preventing the forests' further destruction.[3] We can also provide patrols to protect them and their inhabitants where they are threatened. It is estimated that successfully protecting forests and cutting the rate of deforestation in half by 2030 will save $3.8 trillion globally in environmental costs.[4] Environmental costs are the costs of the actual or potential deterioration of natural assets due to economic activities.[5]

Forests are carbon sinks, and have an economic value as carbon credits in carbon markets. These markets help curtail carbon pollution by placing an economic cost on its generation. In this scheme, companies who create carbon pollution offset their pollution by buying carbon credits, which include forests and renewable energy generation. While there is a voluntary world carbon market in operation, more can be done to ensure that the owners of the forest — whether they are indigenous farmers with partially timbered property or the government — directly receive the funding and use it to protect the forest. Having this income stream reduces the need for deforestation by creating a long-term economic resource for the people living in the mostly poorer countries where the forests are located. We can do more to develop robust national and international carbon markets, which meaningfully contribute to addressing deforestation.

We can also replant native vegetation in a way that mimics the ecosystem that was once there, both to increase the size of existing forests and to rehabilitate damaged areas. In some areas where deforestation has occurred, the soil has been found to be completely unsuitable for agriculture, and returning the land as much as possible to its original state through revegetation is a better use of it.

Other damaged areas are dryland ecosystems, which receive less than twenty inches of rainfall in winter each year and are therefore vulnerable to degradation into desert. A third of all people in the world live and farm in dryland ecosystems, and 70 percent of all drylands are degrading into desert.[6] Globally, we lose an estimated seventy-five to one hundred billion tons of topsoil annually.[7] To halt desertification and erosion, we can plant native vegetation, particularly along waterways and marginal land, but also around villages and farms to create wildlife corridors and improve soil stability. One very successful biodynamic farmer in my area estimates that to look after the land, 5–15 percent of a farm should be under regeneration at any one time.[8] The planting of native trees on farms and in deforested areas can also provide farmers and local communities an additional source of income as carbon credits.[9]

The greater adoption of agroforestry, in which trees are integrated with crops and pastures, can also have a large impact on reducing the vulnerability of dryland ecosystems. Agroforestry:

- restores soil fertility and consequently increases crop productivity
- encourages biodiversity by being able to support an array of insects, birds, and animals and
- depending on the vegetation planted, can provide a source of food, fuel wood, or native medicine.

Replanting native vegetation and adopting agroforestry are ecocentric actions that actively rebuild the web of living systems that support us.

One of the best things we can do to improve food production and rehabilitate the earth is to move to sustainable agricultural systems. These ecocentric systems consider total land management, rather than the produce and environment as in isolation of each other.[10] Sustainable agricultural systems involve a mixture of the following:

- land rehabilitation
- agroforestry
- choosing suitable crops for the local environment
- organic farming
- biodynamic farming
- low-tillage farming
- crop and pasture rotation and
- permaculture for smallholder farms.

Organic farming methods have been found to provide equivalent crop yields to conventional farming under normal conditions, and 24–34 percent more when rainfall was 30 percent less than normal. Organic farming has proven to be both profitable and good for the environment.[11]

Sustainable agricultural systems rely on the use of natural fertilizers and integrated pest management rather than chemical fertilizers, pesticides, and herbicides. There are good reasons for reducing our dependence on farm chemicals. Extended farming on the same area of land coupled with heavy reliance on farm chemicals exhausts the soil and renders the land infertile. This makes the soil vulnerable to erosion.

Farm chemicals were invented in the 1940s, and their use has escalated in the last thirty years. In 2005, it was estimated that more than half the nitrogen fertilizer ever used globally had been used in the previous twenty years.[12] In early 2015, the Food and Agriculture Organization of the United Nations estimated that fertilizer use will rise above two hundred million tons in 2018, representing a 25 percent increase in use from 2008.[13] The excess fertilizer runs into waterways and causes eutrophication, a process in which the excess nitrogen in the water system is taken up by algae, causing them to bloom out of proportion to their normal function in the ecosystem. In doing so, they starve the water of oxygen, causing fish and other riverine animals to die. The chemical pollution in the water also makes it undrinkable for humans.

Pesticide use has also escalated. Pesticides now have ten times the killing power per kilogram and are applied in the United States alone at thirty times the rate as they were in 1945.[14] They are not selective in the insects they kill, and eradicate the pests as well as the useful insects, including the pollinators which keep ecosystems healthy and those that birds eat.[15] Excess pesticide runs off into waterways, rendering the water unusable for other purposes like drinking, bathing, and washing. Some pesticides accumulate in animal fat. This is especially of concern in countries with low or non-existent regulation of pesticide use, as consumption of animals with pesticides in their fat can be hazardous to human health.

In sustainable agricultural systems, organic matter such as animal manure, excess plant matter from crops, and organic waste is used rather than chemical fertilizer. The combination of manure as fertilizer and a three crop rotation has been found to naturally replenish soil fertility, and reduced the need for herbicides and nitrogen fertilizer by almost 90 percent without reducing profits.[16] Organic matter builds the capacity of the soil by returning carbon to the earth, increasing productivity and water retention while reducing erosion and carbon emissions. Its use as a soil improver reinstates a natural cycle, repairing the web of life, and ensuring that the soil can support us into the future. This is a better solution for the earth than burning this material as biomass fuel.

The creation of organic fertilizer is a growing economic venture. Waste management companies around the world are recognizing the value of collecting organic waste in urban centers, turning it into organic fertilizer, and selling it to farmers. This business model is easily replicated, creates jobs, and reduces the burden on local government waste collection services.[17]

Synthetic pesticides are replaced with natural pest management techniques in sustainable agricultural systems. These techniques include crop rotation, timing of planting to avoid high pest population periods, and mechanical weed control.[18] Studies have found that the natural control of pests does not reduce crop yields or increase the price of the crop.[19]

There are a number of things we can do to encourage the shift to sustainable fertilizer and natural pest management techniques. We can introduce a new tax on farm chemicals to discourage their use, the revenue from which can be used to fund advisory centers for farmers shifting to sustainable agricultural systems.[20] Sustainable agricultural systems can be taught in agricultural colleges, with the training incorporating ecology, so that future farmers improve their knowledge of the natural environment and total land management. Governments can also ban the most toxic chemicals, and implement stricter regulations to ensure that safer alternatives are developed by chemical manufacturing companies.[21] These new products will break down rather than persist in the environment, not disperse easily, and not accumulate in animal fat.[22]

The use of water for irrigation is another aspect of farming which negatively impacts the environment. Approximately 70 percent of all water used by humans globally is consumed in the agricultural sector.[23] Traditionally, water has been diverted from aquifer and river systems to agriculture, stressing the natural environment with sometimes devastating effects. A number of irrigating nations are pumping groundwater faster than it is being replenished.[24] Some major rivers do not discharge water into the sea for months at a time. The loss of freshwater flows directly contributes to the extinction of freshwater plant and animal species. In our separateness from our environment, we have been killing the freshwater systems that sustain us.

While we have been damaging our environment by overdrawing water resources for irrigation, approximately 60 percent of the water withdrawn doesn't reach the crop.[25] Traditional surface irrigation methods have been proven to waste water through evaporation and runoff, leading to soil erosion, salinity and farm chemical runoff into nearby waterways. Given that we can expect climate change induced droughts to decrease the amount of water available in many agricultural areas, this situation is not sustainable.

Total land management practices, which consider agriculture and water systems holistically, address this issue. We can improve the health of water systems and produce food by:

- replanting natural vegetation along stream and river banks to slow water flows and reduce erosion
- using organic fertilizer which improves water retention in the soil
- mulching crops to reduce evaporation
- switching to crops which suit the local environment and require less water to grow and
- adopting water saving irrigation methods such as drip irrigation, which use 33 percent less water and have low evaporation rates.[26]

Any infrastructure that has been put in place to direct water flows can be modified to redirect water back into natural systems. These actions make more water available for water systems, improving their health and demonstrating that we are one with the earth.

Sustainable and Humane Consumption of Animals

As part of improving the well-being of all living things on the planet, let's consider how the animals we eat are raised and killed. Have these animals lived with the sun on their backs and the grass underfoot? Have they been treated humanely throughout their life cycle? Animal production has shifted over time to intensive methods, such as large barns for chickens, and feedlots for pigs and cattle to meet increasing demand. While many animals in these production systems are not treated inhumanely, is this the best life we can provide for them? One way we can make a difference to our fellow inhabitants of the earth is to consume less of them, so that those we do farm can roam outdoors.

According to the World Health Organization, in 2014 more than 1.9 billion adults in the world were overweight. Of these, over 600 million were obese. That means that 39 percent of all people aged twenty years and over were overweight, and 13 percent were obese. Over 41 million children under the age of five were also overweight or obese.[27] We can address this epidemic by healing the negative beliefs we hold about ourselves which cause us to overeat, adopting healthy eating patterns, and exercising more. In doing so, we improve our well-being and reduce our consumption of animal products. We can also improve the lives of the animals we consume by insisting on buying meat that has been raised sustainably.

The humane treatment of animals also extends to their deaths. Standards for humane slaughtering practices exist in some countries, but not everywhere. Australia was rocked in May 2011 by demonstrations of cruelty to Australian beef cattle in Indonesian abattoirs, including cattle being dismembered while still alive.[28] Live animal exports were halted for a month while Indonesian abattoirs were inspected, with trade resuming with those that met international standards. The Indonesian and Australian governments and the beef cattle industry have worked together since then to bring additional facilities up to international standards.[29]

The Australian Government also established an Exporter Supply Chain Assurance System which places the onus on meat exporters to ensure that livestock are handled and slaughtered according to World Organization for Animal Health standards, and that the animals can be tracked throughout the supply chain. While the system has not completely prevented further instances of animal cruelty in the live export industry, it has made exporters more aware of their animal welfare responsibilities and enabled action to be taken against negligent exporters.[30] The widespread implementation of systems like this, coupled with greater adoption of World Organization for Animal Health standards in legislation, ensure that animal welfare standards are consistently applied across the world, improving the well-being of the animals we eat.

Sustainable Fishing

Most of us don't think about our impact on the ocean, because we live on the land, and mostly travel by air when we go overseas. Our cumulative impact on it is significant however, and it is close to collapse.[31] As we heal our separateness from the earth, we recognize the important role the ocean plays in our ecological systems and the need to improve its health and the well-being of its inhabitants.

The ocean is home to 50 percent of the earth's species. At the moment, we overfish the world's oceans so much that 87 percent of commercially viable fish species are depleted or overexploited. It is estimated that they will be completely decimated by 2048.[32] Aquaculture contributes to this problem.

Farmed fish are fed fishmeal made from ocean fish at a ratio of three kilograms of wild fish for each kilogram of farmed fish.[33] This situation has been brought about in part by fisheries subsidies of up to $34 billion a year which provide an incentive to overfish.[34]

There are 4.6 million fishing vessels in the world today, but just 1 percent of these take 60 percent of the total catch of approximately ninety million tons per year.[35] These super trawlers drag heavy rollers along the seabed and trail nets big enough to hold several jumbo jets. All the animals and fish that are not wanted are discarded, which amounts to approximately 25 percent of the total catch.[36] These large-scale fishing operations cost ten times as much as small-scale fishing operations and employ 11.5 million fewer people.[37]

Drift nets were outlawed by the United Nations in 1992, because their use caused several marine species other than fish to become endangered. These have been replaced with longlines, which are ropes miles long with thousands of hooks attached. Attracted to the bait, longlines capture sharks, turtles, and birds as well as fish. Another fishing technique which causes enormous damage is bottom trawling, in which the seabed is ploughed up and crushed to stir up the fish. Add to this the drowning of small whales, dolphins, and turtles in nets, and our impact on the ocean environment suddenly seems huge.

To improve the well-being of the ocean's inhabitants, we can address over-fishing and other poor fishing practices by removing all fisheries subsidies, introducing international fishing quotas, and banning super trawlers and longlines. We can also ensure that the fish we eat have been harvested under sustainable principles, such as those established through the Marine Stewardship Council certification scheme. Certification is based on:

- sustainable harvesting
- the maintenance of fish stock health and
- the maintenance of ecosystem integrity, including minimizing the impacts of fishing on marine habitats and non-targeted species.[38]

Poor fishing practices are not the only cause of the negative impact we are having on the world's oceans. Earlier we discussed how excess synthetic farm chemicals run off into waterways, creating water pollution problems. These chemicals are carried out by rivers to the ocean, where they create what are known as "dead zones" that have low levels of oxygen and cannot support life. Nitrogen and phosphorous waste from aquaculture also contribute to dead zones. There are more than four hundred dead zones around the world, with the best known, in the Gulf of Mexico, created by farm chemical runoff in the Mississippi River.[39] The shift to sustainable agricultural systems, and the associated reduction in the use of synthetic farm chemicals, halts the creation of more dead zones.

Our oceans are also polluted by plastic waste dumped on shore and at sea. This waste ends up, due to ocean currents, in huge islands of garbage, some of which are bigger than the state of Texas. The plastic material breaks down into small pieces that seabirds and turtles mistake for food. Consumption of this plastic eventually kills marine animals, because it cannot be digested and remains in their stomachs.[40] As we recognize our connectedness in the web of life, we respect international laws on the dumping of waste at sea and stop polluting our oceans. We can take the opportunity to collect this garbage and recycle it into new products, thereby supporting ourselves while rehabilitating the damage to the earth.

Equitable Distribution of Food

According to the World Food Programme, there is enough food in the world today for everyone, yet over 795 million people go hungry every day.[41] The problem is that it is not equitably distributed, and every year we waste up to 2.2 billion tons — half of all food produced.[42] In an inclusive world, we want everyone to participate in the abundance of the earth. Let's reconsider our food practices and discover what we can do to ensure that everyone has enough food to be able to conduct a healthy and productive life.

People in developed countries have easy access to food through well-established storage, transport, and processing facilities that bring the food from the farm to the supermarket. This supply chain has disconnected us from the earth. Because many of us don't grow food ourselves, we have sometimes unrealistic expectations about how it should look. Those food crops that do not meet our exacting standards are never harvested. Globally, 1.8 million tons of food waste is generated this way every year.[43] As we heal our separateness from the earth, we realize that this food is perfectly edible, and can be eaten either in the country where it is grown or exported for consumption elsewhere.

Many of us buy more food than we can eat, and then throw away between 30 and 50 percent of it.[44] This is an incredible waste of resources. We can address this by:

- healing the negative beliefs we hold which cause us to buy more than we need
- planning our meals so that we only buy what we need and
- composting the organic component of our food waste where possible, so that it is returned to nourish the earth rather than going to a landfill.

While many of us in the developed world are throwing out food, over 795 million people, mostly in the developing world, are going hungry.[45] Droughts in grain-producing countries like Australia, Brazil, and Russia in the last decade, along with rising oil prices, financial speculation on the price of food, and the diversion of food crops for biofuels, have caused global food price rises that contributed to more than 60 food riots in 30 different countries in Asia, Africa, and Central America, and pushed an estimated 130 million people back into poverty from 2007 to 2008.[46]

Between 2006 and 2008, the price of rice rose by 217 percent, wheat by 136 percent, and corn by 125 percent.[47] Global food prices spiked, causing food riots again in 2011, and remain high and increasing.[48] Poor households already spend three quarters of their income on food, so there is no choice but to cut back on the amount purchased, with women and children being the most affected.[49]

As we recognize that everyone deserves to have enough to eat in our inclusive and abundant world, we can address this by building the capacity of developing countries to produce enough food to feed their populations, and have some left over to trade. In rural areas where 75 percent of the world's poor live, most people are involved in agriculture. However, crop yields in many countries are less than 30 percent of the potential yield in currently cultivated areas, leaving developing countries dependent on food imports and aid to meet their food needs.[50]

Much of the world's food needs can be met by improving productivity through sustainable agriculture on small farm holdings, rather than clearing more forest to create farmland. The introduction of sustainable agricultural systems, coupled with the revegetation of forests, marginal, and degraded areas, also improves the resilience of nations to climate change.

A lot of food waste happens in the developing world at the farm end of the supply chain. This is due to inefficient farming methods, inadequate transportation, and poor storage infrastructure, where food frequently spoils.[51] For example, in China, Vietnam, Thailand, and Cambodia, approximately 185 million tons of rice does not reach the consumer each year.[52] Greater investment in agricultural technology, roads, and food storage facilities is required to ensure that the food reaches people both within the country where is it grown and the export market. Food co-operatives also ensure that farmers receive a fair price for their food and have greater access to markets.[53]

This requires greater investment in the protection of forestry and in agriculture than currently takes place.[54] This investment can come from a number of sources. National budgets and international aid can provide a share of the necessary funding and expertise. Carbon credits and the redirection of military spending can also provide investment funds.

Introducing sustainable agriculture on small landholdings in developing countries of course only works where local farmers have small landholdings. Disturbingly, large-scale farmland deals of more than 36 million hectares have taken place since 2000, mostly in Africa, with another 15 million hectares currently under negotiation.[55] These deals, between governments and international investors, occurred in countries with high levels of corruption, weak institutions, and nonexistent laws for the protection of land for local people, and as such, have gone ahead with little public consultation and inadequate compensation for the loss of land rights for local people. These countries have limited capacity to assess a project's technical and economic viability, and limited capacity to enforce the social and environmental protections that may exist.

It comes as no surprise then that poverty and hunger are significantly linked to land rights. It's hard to make a living from agriculture, or continue living in forests as your people have done for generations, when the land has been sold out from under you. The 2005 Millennium Ecosystem Assessment found that the destruction of the environment is a significant barrier to the reduction of poverty, and will be a cause of future poverty and hunger.[56] Further deforestation to produce more food is not the answer to addressing hunger, showing people how to increase their crop yields sustainably is.

Because we are one, we want local people to be able to retain their land, be given their land back, or be compensated for the loss of that land. Where land sales go ahead through free, prior, and informed choice, local people can participate in and benefit from the technological and financial resources generated by large-scale farms. This will generate greater well-being than the current practice of food grown on these farms being exported to developed countries where we throw it out, while the people who live near the farm go hungry. Ways in which local people can benefit include:

- the allocation of a realistic percentage of the land for local use
- the diversion of a reasonable percentage of the crop grown for local use
- the provision of funding and expertise to develop sustainable agricultural projects for local benefit
- employment at the large-scale farms and
- the provision of infrastructure such as schools and hospitals.

We noted earlier that the diversion of food crops for biofuels also contributed to the food crisis. Biofuel production has serious ramifications which cannot continue to be justified given that biofuels have not proven to reduce carbon pollution. The diversion of food products such as corn and wheat to make biofuels reduces the amount of staple food available to feed the world and pushes up the prices of the remaining food. Creating grain-based biofuel uses more energy than the fuel provides, and contributes to deforestation as countries such as Brazil, Indonesia, and Malaysia clear forest to plant biofuel crops. The amount of carbon released into the atmosphere through this deforestation greatly outweighs the amount of carbon reduced through the use of biofuels.[57] A better outcome is to use these crops to feed people, and work on alternate solutions to address climate change, such as electric cars powered from renewable sources.

From an ecocentric world view, all countries can have policies and laws which serve the people and protect the environment. A sustainable food and farming policy, along with supporting legislation, can safeguard the environment and wildlife, stimulate dynamic economic development, and supply healthy food for local markets.[58] Laws in developing countries can:

- protect the rights of local landholders, including the right for women to own land
- protect forests for future generations
- prohibit future large-scale farmland deals and, where possible, reverse existing deals
- ensure that the investors who now own these large parcels of land generate benefits for the local people and
- prohibit the use of land to create biofuels, forcing investment into electric cars and other alternate solutions.

These ecocentric measures reduce our impact on the earth and improve people's access to food, ensuring that everyone has enough to eat. By producing food in harmony with our environment and distributing it equitably, we increase the well-being of all living things, and demonstrate that we are one with each other and the earth.

☙ Key Messages ❧

- By recognizing that everyone deserves to have enough to eat and that we can produce food in harmony with our environment, we increase the well-being of all living things and ensure that the earth can continue to support us into the future.
- Protecting forests, replanting degraded areas, and adopting sustainable agricultural and fishing practices demonstrates that we are one with the earth.

- Reducing food waste and improving people's access to food demonstrates that we are one with each other and the earth.

HEALING THE EARTH

ealing our unsustainable resource use and agricultural and fishing practices will significantly improve the well-being of many people and the earth, but our healing work is not yet complete. We can fully demonstrate our new belief that we and the earth are one by completely healing all human activities which are manifestations of our dominance over the earth. The traditional food, medicine, and exotic pet trade, logging of native forests for paper, mining and manufacturing, and increasing urbanization are next on our list.

To build strong foundations for future generations, we can also modify our existing laws and create new institutions that reflect our appreciation of the earth. In undertaking these activities from our ecocentric world view, we will repair the damage we have done to the web of natural systems we are a part of, and create new ways to support ourselves.

Sustainable Industries

Traditional Food and Medicine, and the Exotic Pet Trade

Many of us like to watch wildlife documentaries on television, but we don't really seem to grasp the danger these animals are in or how rapidly they are disappearing. Approximately twelve thousand animal species are known to be threatened with extinction.[1] While habitat loss plays a major role in their decline, the killing of animals for food and use in traditional medicine, along with the illegal exotic pet trade, have also had a devastating impact on the numbers of animals remaining in the wild, including in our oceans.

Although many species are protected by international and national laws, the demand for illegally traded animals has risen in line with our growing population. The poaching industry is huge and has international security implications. More than thirty thousand elephants are killed each year for their ivory, and illegal fishing is estimated to cost the global economy $23 billion annually.[2] Poaching is now among the top four black markets in the world, with established links to other transnational organized crimes such as drug trafficking, arms running, human trafficking, and money laundering.[3]

Some illegally killed animals are sold for food. The meat of local animals has always been a part of traditional diets in Africa, Asia, and Central and South America. However, increased human populations and shrinking natural habitats have increased pressure on wild animal numbers and are pushing some species, such as gorillas and bonobos, to extinction.[4] Alternative sources of protein are required for people in developing nations to reduce the demand for the meat of local animals. Education campaigns are required to heal people's beliefs about the consumption of endangered species, and to foster local support for habitat conservation and regeneration programs aimed at rebuilding animal numbers to sustainable levels for harvest.

Traditional medicine is used by more than 80 percent of people, or 6 billion of us around the world.[5] Traditional medicine uses animal parts from up to four hundred species as ingredients.[6] The most widely known species used for traditional medicine are the tiger and rhinoceros, but many others, including seahorses and turtles, are also being driven to extinction.

Despite the mechanisms in place to protect endangered species, they are still used in traditional medicine. A 2010 INTERPOL operation targeting the illegal trade in medicines made from protected endangered species, led to arrests across five continents and the seizure of products worth more than $11 million.[7] TRAFFIC, the wildlife trade monitoring network, and the World

Wildlife Fund continue to find traditional medicinal products containing endangered species throughout the world, including in the United States, China, and South East Asia.[8]

The use of wild animal parts by 6 billion people around the world is not sustainable — the animals simply won't last to feed demand. In an inclusive world, we recognize that animals also deserve to exist. We can develop alternatives within traditional medicine to replace the use of their body parts now, before we drive these animals to extinction and are forced to make the change anyway.

Messaging campaigns to heal people's beliefs about the use of animal parts in traditional medicine can be used to sustain the shift. Strengthening and enforcing laws against the use of animal parts in traditional medicine, particularly those from endangered animals, is also important. Western medicine can also be made more available in the developing world, particularly for serious ailments.

The exotic pet trade, and the hunting and wild skin trade, also impact the numbers of endangered species in the wild, particularly big cats, bears, and wolves, but also exotic birds, fish, and reptiles. Healing the use of power will address this situation. We don't need to kill animals, or have them as pets, to feel good about ourselves.

As we live together in harmony, we realize that wild animals are going to be at their happiest and healthiest in their natural environment, with as minimal interference from humans as possible. We can balance our desire to appreciate wild animals with their need for minimal interference, by developing eco-tourism centers that allow people to see animals in their natural environment while keeping some areas completely protected from humans.

While the best way to reduce the demand for wildlife products is by healing our key negative collective belief that we have to struggle to survive, we can also put more resources into stopping their supply. We can use:

- our armies to protect forests
- our navies to protect the oceans
- our intelligence agencies to break criminal networks

- our governments to pass laws protecting forests and oceans, and to increase the penalties for those involved in the illegal trade of animals and
- our justice systems to convict violators.

We can also increase the numbers of endangered species in the wild by undertaking rehabilitation where it is required to improve the health and size of ecosystems.

Forestry

Timber and paper products constitute an important part of daily life for many of us. Indeed, world consumption of paper has grown 400 percent in the last forty years.[9] While some timber and paper products come from plantations, logging for timber and paper products is responsible for 14 percent of global deforestation, and the use of timber as firewood contributes to a further 6 percent.[10] Up to 30 percent of all timber traded globally comes from illegal sources, destroying vital ecosystems in South America, Asia, and Africa.[11]

While our consumption of timber products reduces forests around the world, in many countries the full value of these products is not realized. A good proportion of the billions of trees cut down every year for paper are either flushed down the toilet, or dumped in landfill globally each year.[12] Fortunately, there are a number of things we can do to halt this process and improve the well-being of forests and the communities who live near them.

Firstly, we can cease logging in native forests with a high conservation value, and undertake replanting of native ecosystems where forests have been extensively logged. The cessation of logging requires government investment to diversify local economies, and provide other job opportunities and retraining for people working in the timber felling sector. Where the timber has been used for heating, governments can work with companies and non-governmental organizations to introduce alternative sources of energy, such as the microgrid systems mentioned in Chapter 6, solar lighting, and efficient cooking stoves.

Illegal logging and corruption within the logging industry in developing countries can be addressed with legislation protecting forests, and patrols to ensure laws are being followed. Developing countries can also participate in coordinated international efforts to target the problem, such as the INTERPOL LEAF (Law Enforcement Assistance for Forests) project. This project has successfully undertaken operations against illegal logging, particularly in South America, leading to hundreds of arrests across multiple countries and the seizure of wood worth millions of dollars.[13]

Secondly, we can better manage our timber usage. We can undertake greater recycling of timber products by reusing or repurposing timber furniture, and timber from demolition and building sites. Timber reuse can be incorporated into local building codes and government waste management regulations. We can also use plantation timber from existing Forest Stewardship Council (FSC) and Programme for the Endorsement of Forest Certification (PEFC) certified plantations, and develop long-term FSC certified hard wood plantations on already cleared land. The FSC promotes environmentally appropriate, socially beneficial, and economically viable management of the world's forests through their certification program. We can protect the environment while still supporting ourselves by increasing the number of forests managed under FSC principles. The use of certified plantation timber can also be incorporated into local building codes.

Finally, we can undertake greater recycling of paper products. Approximately 400 million tons of paper and paperboard are produced in the world each year, with recycled paper only accounting for 54 percent of the total.[14] This presents a great opportunity to expand the paper recycling industry across the globe, and make the use of recycled paper products the norm. Governments can help by establishing paper recycling regimes and promoting paper recycling to their citizens.

Given that the demand for toilet paper is increasing with the adoption of western lifestyles around the globe, and this paper is not captured for recycling, we can minimize the number of trees cut down by producing only recycled toilet paper. In addition, governments can develop standards which stipulate that a certain percentage, say 80 percent, of all paper products produced are recycled.

All of these measures can be captured in an integrated timber plan in every country which, with supporting legislation, can be used to:

- protect and rehabilitate the environment
- manage forest resources responsibly
- build timber and paper recycling industries and
- regulate the timber, pulp, and paper industries.

Mining and Manufacturing

Mining and manufacturing create all the products we use every day, but they also create pollution. This pollution is both ecologically hazardous and is a form of economic waste, as it demonstrates that resources have been incompletely or inefficiently used.[15] Pollution can be in liquid, gaseous, or solid form, and is not always appropriately managed.

Pollution has in some instances had adverse impacts on the health of local inhabitants. There are cases of polluted waste streams being discharged into nearby waterways, effectively killing the plant and animal life, and affecting the ability of local people to use the waterways as a food and water source. The discharge of gaseous sulfur dioxide and carbon dioxide causes acid rain and climate change, respectively. Solid waste in developed countries generally ends up in landfill. There have been several instances of hazardous waste not being appropriately treated and disposed of, and then contaminating local soil and waterways, compromising the health of local human and animal populations.

We can change the way we mine and manufacture to reduce the amount of pollution we produce. In Chapter 6, we briefly discussed the adoption of cradle-to-cradle manufacturing, which eliminates waste and pollution by recycling the components of old products into new products, and returning organic material to the soil.[16] Let's explore this holistic, ecocentric method of manufacturing a little further.

We have already established that through the adoption of this method of manufacturing, we will reduce the amount of virgin material required by recycling the components of old products as process inputs. Finding efficiencies in the manufacturing process or modifying processes using new technology, also reduces the amount of inputs, the energy required to manufacture the product, and the pollution produced. The amount of hazardous waste produced can be reduced by using different process inputs that do the same job. This scrutiny and adjustment of manufacturing processes usually results in a reduction of product defects and an increase in profits.[17]

Any waste streams that remain after this process can be contained and used as inputs for other manufacturing processes where possible, to further recycle resources. Uncontaminated organic matter can be used as fertilizer. Where waste streams cannot be used as inputs in other manufacturing processes, they can be treated to remove any hazardous material before being discharged into the environment. The hazardous material can be stored and disposed of appropriately and carefully. Businesses can also reduce their impact on the earth by using energy from renewable sources to manufacture products.

One part of the final product we frequently don't consider is the packaging, which usually ends up in the trash bin. We can reduce the amount of product packaging where it does not provide any health benefits, and ensure that the packaging deemed necessary is easy to reuse, recycle, or compost.[18] Governments can facilitate these changes by providing incentives for industries to shift to cradle-to-cradle manufacturing and renewable energy, and to implement more efficient manufacturing and waste treatment technology. They can also facilitate change by removing subsidies from industries that continue to pollute.

Some level of mining and mineral processing will still be required after cradle-to-cradle manufacturing and greater recycling have been implemented. Mining and mineral processing can also be improved by finding efficiencies or using new technologies to reduce the volume of waste produced. Any waste streams that remain can be contained and used as inputs for another manufacturing process where possible, and hazardous waste stored and disposed of appropriately.

Rehabilitation of mine sites by removing hazardous material, replacing rock and soil material, and replanting native vegetation can commence while the mine is still in operation. Once the mine is closed, rehabilitation can continue to restore the area to as natural a state as possible, and increase the habitat available for local wildlife. Restored sites can also be used as a sanctuary for locally endangered species, increasing our harmony with our natural environment.

Shifting to cradle-to-cradle manufacturing and undertaking greater environmental care when mining will minimize the pollution created in the future, but what about the pollution in the environment that already exists? We can heal the earth by further improving and using technologies that clean up soil and water contaminated by pollution from mining and manufacturing industries. Governments can stimulate improvements in these technologies by providing funding for research and product development.

The rehabilitation and reintroduction of vegetation and animals is a vital part of cleanup operations. The goal of these activities is to return the affected area to the cleanest and most natural state possible, so that the water can be used for drinking and the soil can support forestry or healthy food production. The cost of cleanup is to be borne by the company responsible for polluting the environment, with government incentives to help companies meet this cost. Where the company no longer exists, governments can fund cleanup projects with money previously spent on weaponry, effectively demonstrating the shift to harmony with all living things.

By reforming the industries that create the products on which we depend, we are developing new ways to support ourselves while rehabilitating the damage we have done to the earth, demonstrating that we are one with the earth.

Sustainable Cities

Urban areas also have a huge impact on the environment, but fortunately, there is a lot we can do to address this using sustainable urban development principles. We can stop urban sprawl and infrastructure development in ecologically sensitive areas, such as ocean foreshores, rivers, forests, wetlands, and fens through effective community engagement and the development of robust local government planning processes and laws.

From our ecocentric world view, we recognize that these ecosystems play important ecological functions that can't be replaced. Ocean foreshore vegetation stabilizes sand dunes, and riparian vegetation stops river banks from eroding.

Forests create oxygen, store carbon, and provide homes to native animals. Wetlands and fens are natural water filters, and birthing centers and nurseries for fish and other aquatic animals. These areas can be preserved and turned into low-impact recreational areas for public use.

Sustainable urban development principles can be built into urban planning and development codes to:

- prioritize the revitalization of existing urban areas over the geographical expansion of the city
- stipulate the expansion of urban areas on land that is not ecologically sensitive
- stipulate the development of high- and medium-density housing which is water and energy efficient, and
- permit the adoption of water and energy efficiency measures in existing housing.

Water and energy efficiency measures include:

- grey water recycling tanks, rainwater tanks, and water-saving appliances
- passive solar design principles, which reduce the need for artificial heating and cooling and
- small-scale renewable energy systems.

Government rebate schemes which encourage homeowners to adopt these technologies have proven popular in places where they have been implemented, and are a great way to involve everyone in reducing the city's overall environmental footprint.

All cities have transportation networks and these networks play a large role in the amount of air pollution created. One way to involve everyone in reducing carbon pollution and smog is to provide access for the maximum number of citizens possible to cleanly and efficiently run public transportation. Another way to improve air quality and increase the use of public transportation is to introduce measures that reduce vehicular traffic, such as tolling drivers in central city areas during peak hours. To reduce stormwater runoff, all new roads can be permeable to allow rainwater to flow into the earth. These measures, when combined, greatly reduce the impact of urbanization on the surrounding environment.

Strong Foundations for the Future

A New Regulatory Regime

A natural extension of our healing is to reflect our ecocentric world view in the laws which regulate our society. Providing greater legal protection for the environment demonstrates our understanding of the importance of the web of life, and our reliance on it for our survival. The first and most important regulatory change is to increase the protection of our remaining natural areas from development activity. National parks can be expanded and protected from mining activities, ocean and river fronts can be protected from development, and rivers flowing through dry regions or important forest systems can be protected from damming.

We can also provide greater protection to endangered species, with increased penalties for poaching and smuggling that provide a real deterrent to this illegal trade. Under new laws, anyone seeking to change the status of any natural area through mining, logging, fishing, or urban development for example, has to demonstrate how the value of their activity exceeds the benefit of the natural environment to society as a whole.[19] In this way, we are preserving the environment for future generations.

Business and government can work together to minimize the impact of mining and manufacturing on the environment. Governments provide the legal framework within which business operates, and this framework can be updated to reflect our new belief that we are one with the earth. Our new laws can require mining companies and industrialists to operate under cradle-to-cradle principles, with waste recycled, or properly stored and disposed of appropriately, and include heavy penalties for those who do not comply. Under our new laws, these operators can be required to demonstrate that they have sufficient funds to pay for the mandatory cleanup of any accidental release of toxic material into the environment during operations. They can also be required to provide a significant bond to cover the cleanup and rehabilitation costs of any environmental damage that occurs after operations have ceased.

In addition, they can be subject to audits throughout the life of their operation to ensure that they are complying with the law and any other conditions on their operation. This approach deters investors from risky, environmentally damaging, and unprofitable ventures, and stops the expenditure of taxpayers' money on cleaning up pollution. Adopting strong environmental laws in nations around the globe deters companies who have not healed the belief of their separateness from the earth from shifting polluting operations from one country to another.

As the environment doesn't recognize borders, and the oceans are largely considered to be international waters, we can develop a more comprehensive international legal system that protects the environment as a whole. Countries can work together under the revised United Nations system to develop treaties and bodies to protect areas of environmental significance, whether they are in a single country, cross national borders, or lie in international waters. These treaties can create more forest and ocean reserves, and address:

- deforestation
- poaching
- the sale of land or fishing rights that discriminate against local inhabitants
- illegal fishing in protected areas
- overfishing
- the use of longlines and bottom trawling and
- the disposal of waste in oceans.

To be truly effective, the treaties can include site monitoring, protection, and serious ramifications for those who do not comply.

To enforce these laws, we can provide greater policing, particularly of oceans, and create an international court in which to prosecute offending ruling elites, company executives, or individuals. Developing this comprehensive international legal system is a reflection of our inclusive beliefs, and sends a clear message on the importance of protecting the earth to its human inhabitants.

Technology Transfer Centers

Throughout the last few chapters, we have discussed many ideas which would benefit people all around the world. One of the ways we can ensure this happens is to establish a network of technology transfer centers in developing nations. Through these centers, knowledge and technology can be transferred to developing nations to help them build their economies under sustainable development principles and rehabilitate their environment.[20]

These centers can focus on developing economic and environmental solutions that best suit the local environment and provide long-term, sustainable outcomes for the local people. These solutions include:

- building a sustainable energy base
- transforming agriculture sustainably
- protecting and rehabilitating native landscapes
- introducing cradle-to-cradle manufacturing
- introducing resource recycling centers and
- implementing clean technology for industry.

As with health centers, they can be a collaborative achievement between:

- the governments of developing and developed nations
- international businesses
- universities
- the not-for-profit sector
- the United Nations and
- local people.

Funding can be received from a range of sources, including:

- the Green Climate Fund
- international aid
- the national budget of the country in which they are located
- international businesses and
- research grants.

Building satellite offices in surrounding countries ensures the dissemination of intellectual property, knowledge, and technology as widely as possible.

Technology transfer centers can be staffed by local and international experts, in partnership with national and international universities. Staff can work with national and local governments, local people, and not-for-profit organizations active in the area to determine the body of work the technology transfer centers can undertake in each location. This work can take a range of factors into account, such as the needs and skill base of the population, the local climate, and state of the local environment.

Staff can conduct research to ensure that the solutions implemented in each branch of work are the best suited to local conditions. They can also train local people in the implementation of those solutions, monitor the outcomes, and adjust the solutions as required. By working together in this way, we can provide food and security for all people, reverse the damage we have done to the earth, and bring greater harmony, equality, and well-being to our world.

Rehabilitating the Environment Brings Peace

Technology transfer centers can have a tremendous impact in areas where nations have fought over shared resources. We can create peace by rehabilitating the natural resources that cross boundaries, and developing sustainable sources of income for the countries involved.[21] For example, in areas of water shortage and poor water quality, the staff at the technology transfer centers can work with the governments of all the nations involved and the not-for-profit sector to determine what steps can be taken to improve the quality and quantity of the water for everyone.

The body of work can include:

- reversing water diversion projects
- reducing the pollution entering the water
- introducing low water use agricultural and manufacturing practices
- using technology to clean the water
- replanting riparian zones and forests in the water catchment area with native vegetation to improve the water quality and biodiversity of the region
- reintroducing locally extinct animal and plant species and
- developing alternative industries that do not rely on water, such as sustainable energy generation.

In areas where forests cross national boundaries, staff at technology transfer centers can work with the governments of all the nations involved and the not-for-profit sector to determine the actions to be taken to protect and rehabilitate the forest resource. The body of work may include:

- providing greater legislative and physical protection of the forest
- undertaking replanting programs to rehabilitate damaged areas and extend the forest
- reintroducing locally extinct plant and animal species
- introducing microgrid electricity generation and efficient cooking stoves to reduce the need for firewood and
- developing alternate sources of food and income for local people by improving agricultural sustainability and introducing sustainable industry.

These cooperative efforts build trust and establish collaborative habits which can be sustained well into the future, and create harmony between all living things.[22]

✌ Key Messages ✌

- Reducing our impact on wildlife and native forests, and creating sustainable industries and cities demonstrates that we are one with the earth.
- Providing greater legal protection for the environment demonstrates our understanding of the importance of the web of life and our reliance on it for our survival.
- Working together in technology centers to develop sustainable outcomes builds peace, and demonstrates that we are one with each other and the earth.

Up Next

By taking the actions outlined in this and the previous two chapters, we can actively repair the damage we have done to the earth and create new ways to support ourselves, so that the earth can continue to support us into the future. This is underpinned by our shift in world view from being human-centric to ecocentric, based on the belief that we and the earth are one. For this shift to be complete, and for us to completely heal the world, next we will modify our global economy to ensure that it supports the well-being of all people and the earth.

GREENING ECONOMICS

Traditionally, we have focused our economic activities on creating more money, and have used the amount of money we have as an indicator of how successful we are. Now that we have created new positive collective beliefs, we realize that this definition of success is no longer valid. True success is not measured by money. True success is measured by our individual, collective, and environmental well-being.

The purpose of the economy is to support the society of which it is a part.[1] It is up to us to modify our economy at both the national and international levels so that it best supports us and the planet. At the moment, our economy reflects old beliefs based on separateness, undeservedness, and lack, and does not take into account the impact of our activities on the environment. The first steps to modifying our economy so it reflects our new positive collective beliefs are to redefine the way we measure our success and to incorporate the environment into the economy. We will then consider how governments and business can best support our well-being.

Measuring Success

How we measure our success is important because governments, policy makers, and economists make decisions based on that measurement. We therefore want the measure and the subsequent decisions to reflect everything that is important to us — our individual, collective, and environmental well-being. We also want the measure to be used internationally, so that everyone benefits.

The current measure of economic performance and social progress is the Gross Domestic Product (GDP), which measures the value of the goods and services produced by businesses and government.[2] Growth in the GDP is assumed to mean that we are better off, while a reduction in GDP is assumed to mean that times are hard.

There are a number of inadequacies with this measure across social, economic, and environmental spheres. GDP does not measure actual income and consumption levels, which may be different than the production levels on which the measure is based. While production levels may be high, incomes may at the same time decrease. In this circumstance, people find it harder to make ends meet, which affects their personal well-being. In fact, GDP does not include any consideration of personal well-being and quality of life in its calculation. It also does not consider any work done in the home or voluntarily in the community that is unpaid but contributes to our quality of life.

Because GDP is calculated as an average across a population, it also does not consider the unequal distribution of money. In the United States, in 2015, approximately forty-three million people, or 13.5 percent of the national population, lived below the official poverty line.[3] These people become hidden by the numbers when GDP for the United States is high, yet the unequal distribution of money across society has social impacts on the nation as a whole. GDP also cannot be used as an indicator of long-term economic sustainability. One of the reasons we did not see the Global Financial Crisis of 2008 coming is because the key economic measure we rely on, the GDP, captures only production and not increasing debt levels. GDP is therefore not an accurate indicator of our collective well-being.

In addition, GDP factors in the economic value of all the goods and services that are produced, even if the goods and services produced are not beneficial for society overall.[4] For example, GDP includes the value of the production of weapons and unnecessary packaging. Finally, contributions from the natural environment are not counted in the calculation of GDP. This means that the impact of the loss of environmental resources, which are used to make products and are therefore no longer available for future generations, is not considered.[5]

It makes sense to replace the GDP with another measure that includes social well-being, economic success, and environmental sustainability. The Genuine Progress Indicator (GPI) is the frontrunner to replace the GDP. The GPI uses the GDP as its foundation, but includes the goods and services provided by human and social capital, such as housework, and the benefits of infrastructure and higher education. It adjusts for income inequality, and subtracts negative activity, including environmental costs, the cost of crime, and the loss of leisure time.[6]

So far, consensus on the adoption of this fully inclusive measure has not yet been reached. Let's put our collective energy into this. Adopting the GPI globally provides us with a better basis to judge the overall health of the planet and its people, and we can use it as an indicator of where our attention can be directed to improve well-being.

Incorporating the Environment into the Economy

Another way we can account for the value of contributions from the environment within our economy is to include them in the price of our goods and services. Currently, we assume that natural resources are limitless, free goods. We established in Chapter 6 that we consume our natural resources at an unsustainable rate because of our failure to recognize ecological limits, so the assumption that resources won't run out is false.[7]

The assumption that natural resources are free is also false. We pay a price for all natural resources, but that price includes neither the cost of replacing them, where that is possible, nor frequently the cost of cleaning up pollution. When natural resource replenishment or pollution cleanup does occur, the costs of carrying out these activities are often shifted to taxpayers, rather than the industries that benefited financially from the sale of the natural resources.

Incorporating environmental costs into the products and services that generated those costs is a better way to account for the impact of our pollution and resource use. Environmental costs include the cost of remediating present and future damage to the environment, such as treating and preventing pollution, and accounting for non-renewable resources such as minerals. Including environmental costs can increase the price of goods and services, but the new price is a more accurate indication of the true cost of the good and service. It slows consumerism to more sustainable levels, and shifts consumers to goods and services with lower environmental costs. It also creates an incentive for industries to adopt greater recycling and cleaner production technologies to avoid these costs. Governments can work together to build environmental costs into our financial systems and, by doing so, provide an economic imperative to create new ways to support ourselves within the earth's capacity to support us.

Incorporating environmental costs results in the decline of polluting industries, which can no longer compete economically, and simultaneously encourages the creation of new environmentally friendly industries. For example, the environmental costs for the production of coal generated electricity include:

- accounting for the non-renewable nature of coal
- the costs of pollution control and remediation of coal mines
- the technology used to reduce pollution at coal-fired power plants
- taxes on the carbon pollution that is produced and
- the cost of decommissioning the power plants.

Adding these costs to the current cost of electricity increases the price, creating an incentive for consumers to adopt more energy efficient measures, and for electric companies to move into renewable forms of electricity production. Incorporating environmental costs into our economy therefore helps to protect the environment and ensure that the earth can continue to support future generations.

Another way to account for the contribution of the environment within our economy is to consider the financial value of the services the environment provides to us, in recognition that we and the earth are one. Governments can incorporate, as a matter of standard procedure, the financial value of the environment when making decisions about development applications which impact the earth or the ocean.

For example, with applications to log natural forests, the value of the environmental services the forest performs, such as erosion control, water purification, carbon storage, and homes for indigenous people and animals, can be balanced against the financial value of logging the forest. Usually, the value of the environmental services of any ecosystem easily outweighs the value of using the resources unsustainably.[8] Widespread adoption of this methodology demonstrates our belief that we are one with the earth, as it acknowledges the important functions our environment undertakes to sustain us. It protects the environment from destructive and unnecessary development, and forces businesses to move to sustainable industry models.

The Role of Government and Business in Our Economy

In our global economy, business plays a crucial role in innovating, building wealth, and providing opportunities for meaningful work, while government provides the framework in which business operates. There is a great deal of scope to improve the way the two sectors work together so that our economy best supports us and the planet.

In our current economic system, we have become caught up in the use of power to create money, and have lost sight that the purpose of business and the profit it generates is to contribute to the well-being of society. We have greatly relaxed the regulatory framework in which business and the finance industry operate in order to create growth, which in turn has reduced the accountability of business to society. As we discussed in the last three chapters, we have also failed to legislate effectively to protect the environment from the adverse impacts of business operations. In doing so, we allow businesses to operate in separateness from society and the environment.

International competition exacerbates this trend, with countries cutting taxes and relaxing regulatory standards to attract business investment. Some countries operate as tax havens, where individuals and corporations pay little or no tax. 73 percent of the Fortune 500 companies reported operating in tax havens in 2015, some of them in more than one at the same time.[9] Tax havens perpetuate fraud and political corruption. They also divert funds that should be paid in taxes away from the countries of operation, where companies use the infrastructure provided by governments to operate their businesses.

With our use of power, we have become greedy. Chief Executive Officers (CEOs) and senior executives are paid disproportionately large salaries and bonuses even when companies are failing. In 2015, the CEOs of Standard and Poor's 500 Index of companies were paid 335 times more than the average production and non-supervisory worker - some of whom live below the poverty line.[10]

We are also adversely affecting sustainable business growth by legislating that publicly listed companies return a maximum amount of profits to shareholders. This requirement has led to historically low investment rates and increasing debt, as businesses borrow money to invest into their operations rather than using their profits.[11] This requirement has provided a basis for businesses operating under beliefs based on separateness to justify abuse of laborers and the environment in poor countries in order to maximize profits.[12]

A key reason this has occurred is because we have allowed corporations and other vested interests to have a disproportionate influence in government decision making. In many countries, individuals, corporations, and industry groups bankroll political campaigns and spend millions of dollars lobbying elected representatives.[13] Their considerable financial contributions mean that they have a hold over politicians, which reduces the accountability of politicians to the people who voted for them, and significantly undermines the principles of democracy.

It has gone so far in some countries that lawyers representing corporate lobbies now have significant input into the drafting of legislation to ensure that they get what they want, including the repeal of legislation that regulates them.[14] When this hold over politicians is combined with a failure to undertake long-term planning, governments make decisions that keep corporate money flowing into campaign funds, but which may have long-term detrimental effects on the economy or society as a whole.[15]

The government bailout of the American automotive industry is a good example of government failing to resist pressure from an industry group. The auto industry supplied $15 million in campaign contributions and spent another

$50 million lobbying government in the first nine months of the 2008/2009 financial year.[16] They fought against stricter fuel emissions standards and chose not to develop fuel efficient cars, claiming that Americans want big cars and that any changes to fuel efficiency would result in greater costs.

This inability to anticipate the market and make the changes that were necessary, brought the industry to the point of collapse in the face of competition from Japanese car manufacturers when oil prices escalated.[17] In 2009, the United States government bailed out General Motors and Chrysler with a total of $85 billion to keep the industry afloat.[18]

The US government showed foresight in procuring an ownership stake in General Motors, and in gaining guarantees from the American car industry of developing energy efficient vehicles and consolidating their operations in exchange for bailout funds.[19] However, this situation would never have occurred if the industry had been responsive to changing consumer needs, and if legislation had been in place to curb carbon emissions from cars. If that had been the case, the automotive industry could have spent the money they used to lobby the government on clean technology. Taxpayer money could have been used to provide infrastructure and services to support society, rather than for the bailout.

Similarly, the financial sector's effectiveness in reducing government regulation led to risk-taking behavior in the derivatives market that directly contributed to the Global Financial Crisis (GFC) in 2008. The derivatives market is the market for financial contracts which derive their value from the performance of underlying assets such as stock options or commodities. It is worth more than $600 trillion and was completely unregulated at the time. The US government provided a $180 billion bailout and passed legislation to prevent another such crisis, but the financial sector lobbied hard and somewhat successfully for two years to avoid the regulation of the derivatives market.[20] Their actions very strikingly demonstrate the use of power based on separateness. The GFC had devastating repercussions for people around the world, which the financial sector separates itself from as it attempts to continue operating unchecked.

In 2013, the value of the derivatives market was fourteen times larger than all the stocks and bonds in the world, yet less than 1 percent of trades in the derivatives market were based on the value of actual commodities.[21] Derivatives trades are determined by artificial financial instruments that very few people understand, increasing the risk of volatility in markets. The impacts are large, especially when you consider that we now transfer more money electronically each day through trading than the combined total of all the reserves in the central banks of all highly developed countries.[22] So there are very good reasons to regulate the derivatives market, and the GFC could have been avoided if the financial sector had been adequately regulated in the first place.

Governments Provide the Economic Framework

While there are some inspiring business leaders who are leading the field in incorporating social and environmental responsibility into their operations, most businesses operate within the current economic policy and legislative framework. We therefore cannot expect the market to address environmental destruction and social inequity.[23] It is the role of government to transform this framework to improve the well-being of the planet and its people.

Changes in economic policy need not mean that economic health is sacrificed. We can expect growth in environmentally friendly industries and low-impact services, for example.[24] It does mean that we have to abandon the idea of growth for the sake of growth, where it does not translate into improvements in our collective and environmental well-being. This is why we need economic indicators that capture our overall well-being.

Government interference has been strongly discouraged in our current neoliberal, free market system. However, throughout history governments have always improved their economic policies to drive the change that was required at the time, and this situation is no different.[25] Governments can demonstrate that power is to have inner peace and spread that peace throughout the world, by committing to social, fiscal, and environmental responsibility. They can enact policies and laws through which business, including the financial sector, are answerable to society for the social and environmental impacts of their decisions.

One way to ensure this occurs is to ban political funding from all private sources, including individuals, corporations, and lobby groups. Capped public funds can be provided for campaigning instead.[26] This approach has other benefits besides significantly reducing the undue influence of business on government. The limits of public purse and the need to be accountable for the expenditure of that limited funding will rein in the excesses of political campaigning. To keep within the funding cap, politicians can move away from using expensive television advertising to a radio and internet-based approach to reach the public.

The introduction of long-term planning to meet key societal and environmental objectives also improves government decision making. The policy changes outlined in this book, the building and maintenance of key infrastructure, and the introduction of healthcare and education reforms, require planning and implementation over ten to twenty years and beyond. The development of these plans can be coordinated by a central agency, and their implementation can be debated in parliament throughout this period.[27] Such a system removes quick political fixes for short-term electoral gains.

To be most effective in fully implementing the required structural changes, government policy needs to be harmonized across all government agencies, programs, and departments.[28] This work can also be allocated to the central agency responsible for coordinating the long-term plans. For example, government subsidies for activities that degrade the environment or increase social inequity, can be removed and reallocated to programs that build social well-being, and to the research and development of environmentally friendly technologies. Higher taxes can be applied to the creation of pollution to encourage the adoption of environmentally friendly methods of operation, while reducing the taxation on environmentally friendly business activities.

In previous chapters, we discussed the changes that are required to business operations and legislation to make better use of resources and provide greater environmental protection. If we place greater requirements on business to improve their environmental sustainability, and to undertake rehabilitation of the environment where damage has occurred, then the next step is to amend the law so that businesses can use their profits to invest in technologies that make this possible, rather than returning all profits to shareholders. This can be complemented with favorable tax measures relating to profits that are reinvested in capital.[29] We as shareholders can support this position, as it provides a cleaner and more sustainable future for us all, and reduces the debt burden of the company.

Legislation can also be amended to improve the transparency of the social and environmental impacts of business, international financing organizations, hedge funds, and institutional investors.[30] These organizations can be required to disclose their full impacts around the world, including such things as use of poorly paid labor in substandard working conditions and investment in the destruction of natural habitats, using integrated reporting in their annual reports.[31] This information can be used by companies to demonstrate improvements in their operations over time and help investors to be better informed about the companies in which they choose to invest.

To reinforce social responsibility, and demonstrate the belief that we are one with each other and the earth, governments can:

- increase the minimum wage so that people can enjoy a basic standard of living
- cap corporate salaries and
- cap bonuses to a small percentage of profit, and link them to improvements in the environmental and social performance of the company or financial organization.

Once again, our changes are most effective when they are enacted globally, so that the actions of multinational corporations are transparent no matter where they operate. International cooperation is also required to create a minimum set of operational norms no matter where a business operates. Corporate taxes and financial, labor, and environmental legislation can be standardized so that companies cannot gain at the cost of society or the environment anywhere in the world. A cooperative approach can also be adopted to eliminate tax havens.[32]

One of the agencies in our reconfigured United Nations can provide the forum for countries to come together to set these operating and reporting standards, and develop incentives to eliminate tax havens. This agency can also provide oversight and reporting of the social and environmental performance of multinational corporations, so that member states have an accurate picture of what is occurring globally and how changes in environmental and corporate reporting legislation impact corporate behavior over time.

What Business Can Do

The business and financial sectors can contribute to the well-being of the planet and its people by incorporating social, fiscal, and environmental responsibility into all of their operations, and by being active in encouraging other businesses to do the same. Some are ahead of the game. They have recognized that creating profit and contributing to the well-being of society and the environment are not mutually exclusive. They have established overarching principles in corporate, social, and environmental responsibility charters, and have imbedded these principles into all aspects of their operations.

These organizations recognize that a socially and environmentally responsible reputation helps them win business. They use their creativity to generate new products that support our human and environmental well-being and reach new markets.[33] They use their market position to generate change through their supply chain by ensuring that suppliers also meet labor and environmental standards.[34] They actively demonstrate that power is to have inner peace, and spread that peace throughout the world.

CEOs can follow these leaders and spread peace by fully integrating social, fiscal, and environmental responsibility into all aspects of their operations. They can show leadership within their own organizations by being active in undertaking these measures, rather than waiting for change to be forced upon them by legislation, or because of bad publicity about their operations generated by concerned non-governmental organizations and members of the public.

They can start with a full social and environmental audit of their operations, then eradicate damaging policies and operations, and replace them with socially and environmentally empowering practices. They can direct their profits into adopting cradle-to-cradle manufacturing, renewable energy generation, and innovating sustainable products and service delivery methods. They can adopt salary caps and link bonuses to improvements in social and environmental well-being. In doing so, they will ensure their ongoing competitiveness into the future, and will find that helping others and the environment, as part of business, is far more satisfying than just making money.

Businesses can also demonstrate the shift to positive beliefs by ceasing their use of tax havens and their lobbying of governments to retain outdated policies. Instead, by working with governments to improve our collective and environmental well-being, they can demonstrate that power is to have inner peace and spread that peace throughout the world. They can contribute to society by building corporate, environmental, and social best practice into their industry, and financially through taxes to the physical and social infrastructure of the countries in which they operate. They can also develop an international tax haven free certification program with a recognizable logo, so that consumers can easily identify which companies are contributing to society through their taxes.

Over eight thousand businesses and four thousand other organizations in over 162 countries have demonstrated their commitment to social and environmental responsibility by joining the UN Global Compact. Through this initiative, which is designed to complement regulation, participants voluntarily align their operations and strategies with ten principles in the areas of human rights, labor, environment, and anti-corruption. All participants regularly report their progress towards these principles.

The UN Global Compact is a good resource base for businesses with little history or knowledge of social and environmental responsibility. In addition, participants are linked with other businesses as well as UN agencies, governments, and civil society to create sustainable solutions through partnerships.[35] This approach recognizes the importance of working together and learning from each other across different sectors to further social and environmental sustainability, and create our peaceful planet.

Key Messages

- True success is measured by our individual, collective, and environmental well-being.
- Incorporating environmental costs and services into our economy demonstrates that we are one with the earth by reflecting the value we place on the web of life that supports us.
- Governments and business working together with a common commitment to social, fiscal, and environmental responsibility demonstrate that power is to have inner peace, and spread that peace throughout the world.

EQUALIZING ECONOMICS

n 2013, 2.3 billion people — 32 percent of the world's population at that time — lived on less than $3.10 a day.[1] Some people always lose in a global economy that reflects our key negative collective belief that we have to struggle to survive, played out through the use of power and identity. Their struggle to survive leaves them starving, open to exploitation, and amenable to crime and corruption and the idea of fighting those who have more. In our inclusive world, we want everyone to be able to live freely and participate equitably. We want everyone to enjoy a decent standard of living, and have the dignity of legitimately supporting themselves through their skills and labor, while living in harmony with the earth.

Fortunately, there is a lot we can do to lift people out of poverty and spread peace, economic development, and environmental protection throughout the world. While trade and aid play important roles in this, we can also modify the way our international financial institutions and systems are structured, so that all nations can participate equitably in our global economy. By working together to build socially and environmentally sustainable economies in developing nations, we will improve the well-being of people and the environment around the world. In doing so, we demonstrate that power is to have inner peace and spread that peace throughout the world, and that we are one with each other and the earth.

Free and Fair Agricultural Trade?

At the moment, there are a number of barriers to economic development in developing nations. War and corruption, which we discussed in Chapters 4 and 5, are two important ones. The inequity in our current trade system is another. Our negative collective belief that we have to struggle to survive is played out through the use of power and identity in trade policies, and the institutions we have established to negotiate trade agreements. Wealthy nations use power to further their own means at the expense of others, and use identity to work in blocs against poor countries, with poor countries having insufficient influence on the international stage to make a significant difference in the well-being of their people.

The agricultural trade policies of China, Japan, the European Union (EU), and the United States are good examples of this. While agriculture only forms a relatively small proportion of the overall economy in developed nations, many developing nations rely on the sale of goods from primary industries like agriculture to support themselves. Yet some developed and emerging nations use their wealth to subsidize their agricultural industries through government funding, and gain an advantage in the global marketplace by doing so. In 2012, China spent a massive $165 billion on agricultural subsidies, while the EU spent around $106 billion to subsidize the production of most agricultural products, including wine and dairy. Japan spent $65 billion, while the United States spent approximately $30 billion to subsidize key export crops including cotton, corn, soy, and rice.[2]

The impact of these subsidies can be demonstrated using the cotton trade. An average of $2 billion a year is spent by the United States on subsidies for cotton.[3] Growing cotton in the United States costs more than three times what it costs in poor nations.[4] Because farmers receive more subsidies the more they grow, they overproduce. The excess stock is then dumped on the world market, lowering world prices to less than what it costs to produce the cotton in developing nations without subsidies.[5]

Subsidies give western farmers an unfair advantage developing nations cannot compete with, and drive farmers in developing countries into poverty. Not being able to sell their crops at what it costs to produce them, leaves farmers in developing countries with three options: they can clear forests to grow more of an agricultural product in order to make a living, they can go deeper into debt, and cut back on household costs like food or education for their children, or they can leave farming altogether and move to the city. The net effect is:

- wide-scale destruction of rainforests in tropical countries
- a reliance on imported staple foods that they could grow themselves
- fewer children receiving food and education and
- wide-scale migration to cities, which increases poverty in urban areas.

The situation is worsened by financial speculation on the agricultural commodity derivatives markets, which adds to the volatility of food prices. People in developing countries are unable to afford imported food when prices are up because of speculative commodity trading, and growers are forced to sell their crops for less than what it costs to produce them when prices are down.

Wealthy nations argue that without subsidies, western farmers are not able to compete in the world market against farmers in developing countries, where the cost of labor is much less. They claim that subsidizing farmers is the only way to preserve the tradition and landscape of farming in their countries, which some consider a vital part of their national identity.

However, in these countries, farming has changed over the years from family farms to big business. The reality is that the largest 10 percent of farmers and agribusinesses in the United States receive approximately 75 percent of the subsidies.[6] Similarly in Europe, the bigger you are the more money you get.[7] So rather than keeping small farmers on the land, subsidies are mostly benefiting large agribusinesses, which is counter to what subsidies are meant to do. In free market economies, businesses are supposed to be able to function without handouts from the government.

Subsidies are accompanied by tariffs in developed countries. Tariffs are taxes imposed on imported agricultural products and manufactured goods to make them more expensive than goods produced domestically. This encourages consumers to support domestic industries through their purchases. While tariffs are designed to protect local farmers and businesses, they create a further barrier for developing nations who cannot export their goods for a fair price. Subsidies, tariffs, and financial speculation in the agricultural commodities market stop developing nations from being able to participate equitably in the global economy.

Nations discuss reducing subsidies and tariffs to free up trade through the World Trade Organization (WTO). The WTO also promotes the rules of trade and mediates disputes between nations over trade practices. The most recent round of world trade negotiations have had limited success to date. The Doha Round commenced in 2001, and has not yet been finalized because nations cannot come to an agreement, principally on the removal of agricultural subsidies. This round of talks is also known as the Development Round, as it is supposed to focus on the opening of markets in developed countries to products from developing countries. Since wealthy nations work in blocs against developing nations in this forum, this has not yet happened.

There are other issues with the functioning of the WTO besides a lack of progress on trade negotiations. The WTO was established to facilitate free trade, and its rules reflect this role. In cases where countries have tried to raise health, safety, labor, or environmental standards in other countries through trade, they have been taken to dispute resolution by the country with lower standards and have lost. These standards include measures to protect forests, eco-labeling and energy efficiency ratings, and the regulation of toxic chemicals that affect the health of workers.[8] In these cases, the WTO has ruled that the country with higher standards is practicing trade protectionism, which means it is trying to protect its own manufacturers from competition from overseas manufacturers.

The WTO is able to make this ruling because very frequently the countries that are trying to raise standards overseas have not consistently applied those higher standards across the relevant industry in their own country. While the outcome of the ruling does show flaws in the application of standards in the first country, it also impedes the adoption of measures to improve labor standards and environmental sustainability across the world.

A New Era for Agricultural Trade

With the existence of subsidies, tariffs, and agricultural commodities markets being open to speculative trading, agricultural trade is no longer a matter of supply and demand, and certainly is neither free nor fair. Let's go back to our principles of inclusion, deservedness, and abundance. For the well-being of everyone to be high, we all need to be able to feed ourselves. There are a number of ways we can achieve this. First and foremost, as we discussed in Chapter 7, this involves improving the capacity of developing countries to produce their own food sustainably, so they are not reliant on food imports.

Next, to demonstrate that power is to have inner peace and spread that peace throughout the world, developed countries can phase out agricultural subsidies and tariffs, leveling the playing field for developing nations. This doesn't mean that developing nations become the food bowl for the world. Sound policy is for each country to sustainably produce food for its own people, export the surplus, and import the additional food that it needs or those items which cannot be grown because of the local climate. This will mean that some key crops, like cotton and rice, will probably shift to developing countries with the right climate and growing conditions, where they can be produced more cheaply.

While there have been calls for greater regulation of agricultural commodity derivatives trading to minimize food price volatility, this doesn't go far enough. Should we really be playing with agricultural commodity derivatives at all, if it means that someone won't be able to afford to eat? We can ensure that financial trading does not manipulate the prices of agricultural products with legislation limiting their trade on commodity markets to legitimate buyers and sellers of agricultural products only. This still leaves a number of other products (including oil, energy, metals, and minerals) open to financial speculation on commodity markets, but it protects people's well-being from the negative impacts of financial speculation.

With the removal of agricultural subsidies, tariffs, and food products from commodity derivatives speculation, in theory, the price of food in a free market should reflect the amount of supply and demand. While a situation of oversupply drives down prices and is an incentive for farmers to switch to more profitable crops, it runs the risk of maintaining poverty for farmers in poor nations who frequently do not have access to the seeds of other crops and lack the knowledge to grow them. Technology transfer centers can play an important role in addressing this situation, by introducing alternate crops suitable to the local climate, educating farmers about their sustainable production, and facilitating the development of agricultural infrastructure.

We can implement these measures through a new international agreement on agriculture, negotiated through the reconfigured United Nations. The goal of the agreement can be making sure that everyone has enough sustainably produced food to eat, and that trade in agriculture is free and fair. This agreement can then form the legal basis for future agricultural trade negotiations in the WTO, and for the limits placed on who can trade on the agricultural commodities market.

To reflect our inclusive beliefs and play its role in socially and environmentally sustainable development, the WTO can change its core function from freeing up trade to improving social and environmental well-being through trade. It can update its rules to ensure that labor and environmental standards are included in all trade agreements.[9] Countries that deliberately abuse laborers and the environment to create cheaper products can then be taken to dispute settlement, providing another forum to address and eliminate practices based on separateness, undeservedness, and lack. By implementing these measures, we can stabilize income for farmers in developing countries, provide sustainably produced food for everyone, and improve the well-being of people and the environment, demonstrating that we are one with each other and the earth.

Why Are Some Countries Poor?

While agriculture is critical for our survival, countries must be able to export other products and services as well in order to lift people out of poverty and create greater harmony and well-being in the long term. To do this, countries need socially and environmentally sustainable economies that operate under good governance principles, and enhance the human and natural capital of the nation.

Sound macroeconomic policy is to have three sectors present in a national economy: primary industries such as agriculture and mining, secondary industries such as processing and manufacturing, and tertiary service industries such as telecommunications and tourism. Most developing countries rely on primary industries. Some have small manufacturing industries and others have telecommunications and tourism industries. A small number rely on criminal activities, including drug production and trafficking, the sex trade, child and slave labor, and arms and human trafficking. Some countries have almost nothing and rely on international aid to survive.

It seems obvious that the way to ease poverty in developing nations is to help them build all three sectors in their economies. In developed countries, economic development happened over centuries and with a great deal of pollution. In today's world, with the rapid expansion of telecommunications and environmentally friendly technology, developing countries can build all three sectors simultaneously without further damaging the environment.

So why hasn't this happened so far? There are a number of reasons. Firstly, many developing countries owe huge debts to the World Bank, International Monetary Fund (IMF), and western governments through export credit agencies. In 2014, developing countries owed a massive $5.4 trillion. The top ten borrowers, including countries like China and India, are responsible for approximately 70 percent of that debt, leaving other developing nations with a combined debt of around $1.6 trillion.[10]

Both the World Bank and the IMF were established, along with the UN, after World War II and both lend money to nations. The World Bank provides loans to developing countries for capital programs like building infrastructure, while the IMF provides loans to help countries out of financial difficulty or to fight poverty. The IMF is also responsible for promoting exchange rate stability and international trade, and provides economic advice to countries. Although created as part of the UN system, both institutions now tend to operate in isolation of it. The IMF has been criticized by world leaders and academics for being too closely aligned with international banks to be able to provide objective and independent advice, and for having a voting system on policies weighted in favor of developed countries.[11]

Export credit agencies provide government backed loans, credit guarantees, and insurance to corporations based in their home country seeking to do business with nations who have a bad debt record or high-risk political profile. They are the largest sources of official financing for projects in developing countries, and have weak frameworks for considering the social and environmental impacts of projects when making funding decisions.[12]

In the past, developing countries have borrowed money purportedly for development projects, but in displays of the use of power and identity, the funds disappeared into the overseas bank accounts of corrupt government officials, were spent on military programs, or wasted on poorly conceived projects. The money did not reach the people through public spending, nor was it used to build industries in a way that provided jobs and raised the overall standard of living.[13] The debts incurred of course still have to be paid by successive governments, which is hard for impoverished countries with small export industries and taxation bases to do.

Secondly, rather than considering how to best build sustainable economies, for many years the World Bank and IMF gave unsound policy advice which has worsened the situation. Demonstrating the use of power and identity, both institutions instructed developing countries to increase their export earnings through the sale of cash crops and natural resources such as timber, in order to pay off their debts. The result has been the destruction of forests through logging and clearing for agriculture, the displacement of small sustainable farmers into cities, and an overall increase in poverty and malnutrition.

The sale of these commodities was impacted by oversupply created by subsidies in developed countries, and fluctuations in the world market, ultimately lowering returns. This advice established a destructive precedent that is still being followed by many countries. While some debt has been repaid, it is at the cost of manufacturing and service sector development, and the supply of public services including health, education, and infrastructure.[14]

The IMF and World Bank continue to insist on a number of structural reforms in the economies of developing nations as part of the loan conditions. These reforms include balancing the budget, exchange rate reforms, privatization of public services, and opening up internal markets to foreign investment. While these reforms seem reasonable, in reality they have caused recessions leading to mass unemployment, some corrupt international business deals, and the theft of public funds by corrupt politicians. This demonstrates that economic reforms are only effective when they take place in conjunction with the healing of negative beliefs and broader governance and social policy reforms.[15]

Thirdly, conflicting aid and trade policies also impede development in poor nations.[16] Developed countries gave a total of $135.2 billion foreign aid in 2014.[17] That works out to be a total of $23 per person receiving the aid. At the same time, the top food-producing nations spent over $486 billion, more than three times the amount of aid given, to protect their agricultural sectors. They also continue to have tariffs against imported food and manufactured products.[18]

In 1970, at the UN, developed countries set a target of 0.7 percent of their Gross National Income (GNI) for official aid funding. Since then, in a demonstration of separateness, undeservedness, and lack, total aid has been between 0.2 percent and 0.4 percent of GNI, producing a significant shortfall of $159 billion a year.[19] This aid frequently comes with strings attached, like a condition that the funding recipient must buy goods and services from the donor country which can be sourced more cheaply elsewhere.[20]

This shortfall in funding extends to some UN agencies, which perform critical tasks in developing countries. All member countries financially contribute to the UN, however, the World Food Programme and UNICEF do not receive funding out of the regular UN budget. They are instead funded by private donors and voluntary contributions from individual member governments who may be unable to pay during economic recessions. In 2009 and again in 2015, the World Food Programme had to cut services because insufficient funding was received.[21]

Despite the shortfall in aid funding, there are a large number of players providing development assistance. The World Bank and the IMF play a role in economic development, and individual donor countries have bilateral aid arrangements with recipient countries for disaster relief and poverty alleviation projects. Charities also run programs in developing nations. In separateness, these players frequently work in isolation of each other, often without a strategic plan and sometimes towards opposing goals. They implement thousands of disaster relief and poverty alleviation projects, many without sufficient funds to achieve long-term, sustainable outcomes. This chaotic system also places an administrative burden on developing nations as they fulfill the reporting requirements of each UN and bilateral project to demonstrate that the funds given have produced outcomes.[22]

Finally, it must be acknowledged that some countries have developed a dependency on aid based on negative collective beliefs. These countries use aid to prop up their economies, rather than to become self-empowered.

So in response to our earlier question, we now know that some countries are poor because they struggle with:

- high debt levels
- poor advice from international monetary institutions
- trade protectionism by developed nations
- poorly funded and coordinated aid and
- negative collective beliefs which keep them dependent on aid.

With so many factors based on separateness, undeservedness, and lack, it is little wonder that these nations struggle to lift themselves out of poverty.

Building Socially and Environmentally Sustainable Economies

Fortunately, there is a lot we can do to build socially and environmentally sustainable national economies that support the well-being of people and the environment around the globe. By working together across governments, the private sector, and non-governmental organizations, we can end poverty and enable everyone to participate equitably in our world. Our actions will demonstrate that power is to have inner peace and spread that peace throughout the world, and that we are one with each other and the earth.

A Ten Year Plan to Build Healthy Foundations

Leaders of developing countries, with peace in their hearts, can be courageous and visionary in developing the democratic and economic foundations for a thriving, happy, and economically self-sustaining societies. In these societies, everyone can enjoy a decent standard of living and have the dignity of legitimately supporting themselves financially through their skills and labor, while living in harmony with the environment.

The first step towards this is for leaders of developing countries to produce a ten-year plan outlining how they will:

- create the positive collective beliefs which underpin prosperity, social cohesion, and self-empowerment
- create peace
- build good governance
- introduce laws to protect vulnerable people from exploitation
- protect and rehabilitate the environment
- eradicate crime and corruption
- educate the population
- create the economic conditions in which environmentally sustainable businesses in all three sectors can flourish
- build a taxation base and
- eliminate their country's reliance on foreign aid.

While this seems like a long list, these factors are interrelated and work together to create healthy foundations for long-term peace and prosperity.

The plan can also include the country's public investment priorities:

- health and technology transfer centers
- poverty alleviation and environmental restoration projects and
- infrastructure, such as roads, schools, food storage facilities, water and sewage treatment, roads and ports, recycling facilities, renewable energy, and telecommunications.

The plan can also stipulate that infrastructure be distributed around the country for equitable access by all people, and be built using sustainable principles and recycled materials where possible.

If the construction of this infrastructure is to be put to international tender, the plan can stipulate that international companies interested in implementing the project be required to work in partnership with local companies, source a large percentage of the workforce from the local population, and provide training to build the local knowledge and skill base.

Aid funded international experts can work with leaders in developing countries to create their socially and environmentally sustainable economic plans, if required, and help them identify and agree upon immediate and long-term funding priorities. The plan can then be made open to public consultation with local businesses and non-governmental organizations, so that the changes required in building the direction of the country have ongoing local support.

Having a ten-year plan and being committed to it creates investor confidence, which is necessary because building socially and environmentally sustainable economies requires collaboration between the public and private sectors. Technology transfer centers can be expected to play a significant role in building socially and environmentally sustainable economies. Domestic businesses may be encouraged through microfinance schemes, which provide financial services to low income earners. International companies can bring their funds and ideas to create new business. The presence of these businesses leads to increased corporate and household incomes and savings, which in turn provide a source of tax revenue for the host government and form the basis of a self-sustaining economy.

Paying for the Implementation of the Plan

No economic plan is complete without an estimate of how much money is required to fulfill it, and an understanding of where that money will come from. Keeping in mind that the purpose of the plan is to build self-sustaining economies, it's important to outline the circumstances under which borrowing further funds is acceptable and when it is not. After all, there is no point getting further into debt. It is always better to pay for things out of your budget first, and only borrow money when you can afford the repayments.

Once the economy starts developing, increased tax revenue and reduced spending on military programs in our peaceful planet will certainly help the bottom line, but this in itself will not produce enough money to fully implement the plan. Debt cancellation, and changes in trade arrangements and aid are also required.

It becomes impossible for developing countries to get ahead with such high levels of debt. Developed nations have to bear some of the responsibility since their own credit arrangements, as well as the advice given through the World Bank and the IMF, have worsened rather than improved the situation. In our inclusive world, we realize that the best thing we can do to demonstrate that we are one, is to cancel the debt.

The 2005 Make Poverty History Campaign, which millions of people across the globe supported, provides a precedent for debt cancellation. The campaign resulted in $36.9 million of debt relief for the world's forty poorest nations, who were able to spend the money previously being channeled into debt repayments on initiatives that stimulated economic growth and reduced poverty, including providing free healthcare and primary school education.[23] However, many of the promises made in response to that campaign were structured in favor of developed nations and have not been upheld. The poorest developing countries still have a combined debt of $1.6 trillion.[24]

We can cancel this debt in a fair and transparent international process on the condition that developing countries create and implement a ten-year plan as outlined above. The poorest countries can be eligible for full debt cancellation, while those countries with more advanced economies that can manage smaller debt repayments can receive partial cancellation.

Debt cancellation can occur over a period of time in line with the implementation of the ten-year plan. Partial debt cancellation can occur when particular milestones have been reached, such as when indebted countries submit their plans and when they demonstrate transparency and accountability in the use of public money. Debt repayments may be suspended or reduced to empower developing countries to at least partially fund the implementation of their plans from their own budgets. Full debt cancellation can occur when the country can demonstrate that the necessary democratic and economic changes have been embedded into their society and maintained for a period of ten years.

To enable developing countries to participate equitably in our global economy and effectively build sustainable economies, debt cancellation can be accompanied by changes in trade policies by developed nations. In addition to the abolition of agricultural subsidies and tariffs discussed earlier, developed nations can remove tariffs against imported manufactured goods from developing countries.[25] Service centers and processing facilities for minerals, agricultural products, and recycling materials can then be established in developing countries with the knowledge that they can sell their goods and services in a truly open market. In our inclusive world, we want everyone to succeed.

For some countries, even full debt cancellation will not provide them with enough funds to stimulate their economies and invest back into their own countries through public services and infrastructure. Aid can help developing countries to build sustainable economies, but changes to the funding and the coordination of projects are required for aid to be sustainable and fully effective.

Effective Aid Implementation

We have already noted that there is a shortfall in aid funding. Debt cancellation is also an expensive business. The IMF used the proceeds from the sale of its gold stocks to fund its portion of debt relief from the Make Poverty History campaign, which is not a sustainable ongoing strategy.[26] With many countries experiencing economic constraint following the Global Financial Crisis, promises to increase aid funding are not likely to be met.[27] More sustainable funding sources are required.

In 1978, James Tobin, a Noble Laureate economist from Yale University, proposed a tax on currency transactions to dampen short-term speculation that can cause significant economic problems for countries. His proposed tax would stabilize exchange rates, but would be low enough to not have a significant effect on longer-term investments.[28] His analysis on the impacts of short-term speculation remains pertinent today. Only 5 percent of currency transactions are for trade or other aspects of the real economy. The remaining 95 percent are made by speculators who profit from exchange rate fluctuations by moving large volumes of money around the world.[29]

Tobin suggested that the tax be applied at a rate of 0.5 percent of the volume of the transaction, and be administered by each government over its own jurisdiction, with the proceeds of the tax going to the IMF or World Bank.[30]

For example, in 2012, the tax would have raised approximately $5.7 trillion if it had been applied.[31] That amount of money is more than enough to address debt cancellation and the shortfall in funding for aid, and can also be used for international environmental restoration projects.

The money raised from the Tobin Tax is to supplement, not replace, the aid funding currently pledged by nations. Indeed, in our inclusive world, the regular UN budget can be increased to fund all UN agencies, and this can only be paid for by increased member contributions. Beyond increased payments to the UN, individual nations may like to reconsider how to achieve the best outcome for developing countries from their aid funding. Rather than having bilateral arrangements with recipient countries, they can give their aid funding to the UN or World Bank for distribution to gain the maximum effectiveness from consolidated aid funding.[32] They can also provide aid in the form of international expertise to support governments or health and technology transfer centers, and scholarships and exchange programs to educate people in the universities of the developed world.

Earlier we discussed some of the issues with the current operation of the IMF and World Bank. It's time to realign the functions of both institutions so that they remain relevant and useful in our peaceful planet. We can bring them within the UN system once again, so that they can work closely with other UN agencies, and report to the Secretary-General of the UN. We can also change the constitution of their boards and their voting policies to include developing countries, enabling these countries to participate equitably.

The core function of the IMF can become to ensure that international finance produces socially and environmentally sustainable outcomes. It can:

- stabilize the global monetary system by monitoring and regulating the capital flows, particularly short-term bank loans, portfolio flows such as hedge funds, and derivatives
- develop and apply rules for all international investment and financing facilities, such as export agencies and development banks, to ensure that funded projects are socially and environmentally sustainable and
- provide loans to creditworthy countries in short-term financial difficulty.

The money raised from the Tobin Tax can be transferred by each nation to the World Bank, along with aid funding from donor countries. The World Bank is then responsible for distributing the funds:

- for debt forgiveness
- through grants to developing countries to build their infrastructure, rehabilitate their environment, and reduce poverty as outlined in their ten-year plans. Depending on the economic circumstances of the recipient country, the World Bank may seek a financial co-contribution for some projects to demonstrate commitment to their implementation.
- to health and technology transfer centers in developing countries on an ongoing basis
- to projects developed under environmental treaties and
- for disaster relief.

There are a number of notable differences between this model and the current situation. In this model, the funds raised through the Tobin Tax are dedicated to creating our peaceful planet, and not diverted into projects in developed or emerging economies.

In addition, neither the IMF nor the World Bank can provide economic advice. As long as the developing country is building a mixed economy based on sound theory, and the ten-year plan includes all the listed elements, then funding can be granted. So that the World Bank can be satisfied that the funds provided contribute to long-term peace and prosperity, developing countries are to demonstrate their progress in implementing all elements of their plan, even if they are seeking aid funding for only one element.

By tying the allocation of grant funding to the ten-year plans, we are paying for projects based on the needs of the recipient country, rather than having donor directed decision-making. This system also allows the government of the developing country to build their capability in advancing their country and managing their budget, and significantly reduces the administrative burden of reporting to multiple funding sources.

The UN can play a pivotal role in the planning and coordination of aid in recipient nations. Rather than having each UN agency present and working in isolation of other agencies, there can be a senior UN representative in each developing country. They can be responsible for designing a country-specific program for the total expenditure of UN funds in that country in line with its ten-year plan, and for delivery of all UN programs in that country. Staff from each agency in our reconfigured UN can report to and work with that senior representative, who in turn can report directly to a Deputy Secretary-General.[33]

Charities may wish to continue funding specific projects directly. However, they will have the most impact by working closely with the senior UN representative and the government of the developing country to ensure that their projects align with that country's plan for socially and environmentally sustainable economic development. This inclusive approach reduces duplication of effort, and better ensures the achievement of long-term sustainable outcomes.

Governments, businesses, and charities all have a role to play in ending poverty. By contributing to the realization of each developing country's ten-year plan, and making the requisite changes to aid funding and delivery through our international institutions, we can ensure that it happens in a coordinated way that delivers results. As countries build socially and environmentally sustainable economies, they eliminate their need for aid. We can then redirect this funding into health and technology transfer centers, to projects developed under environmental treaties, and to disaster relief. Together, we can improve the well-being of people and the environment by spreading peace, and building socially and environmentally sustainable economies around the world. Together, we can demonstrate that power is to have inner peace and spread that peace throughout the world, and that we are one with each other and the earth.

༄ Key Messages ༅

- Developed countries demonstrate that power is to have inner peace and to spread that peace throughout the world by making the changes required to enable developing countries to participate equitably in our global economy.

- Developing countries demonstrate that power is to have inner peace and spread that peace throughout the world by building thriving socially and environmentally sustainable economies.
- We demonstrate that we are one with each other and the earth by working together to build socially and environmentally sustainable economies in developing nations around the world.

PART 3

TOGETHER WE CAN ACHIEVE AMAZING THINGS

THE FUTURE

hat will our planet look like when we have implemented the actions outlined in this book?

On our peaceful planet . . .

. . . we actively heal our negative individual and collective beliefs on an ongoing basis. Through this healing, our perspectives of ourselves, others, and the earth shift to become loving, accepting, and holistic, and we take actions which reflect our new beliefs. We are at peace within ourselves. We accept that though we may look different and come from different places, we are the same. We respect each other. Our family relationships are strong and caring. Communities share resources, support each other, and look after their local environment.

. . . we create societies in post-conflict zones that are structured to enable harmonious, meaningful, and equitable participation where people want to return and live. People vote, work, learn, and live peacefully in their communities, knowing that they are all equal and all belong. The well-being of millions of people increases, contributing to the long-term peace and stability of the world.

. . . people everywhere live peacefully and free in democratic societies where they are safe, and in which they can equitably and meaningfully participate. We keep minimal stocks of weapons because we live in harmony with each other. People respect each other and their well-being is high. We all equitably participate in the economy of our nations. We work together to create and sustain peace, and human and environmental well-being through an effectively structured United Nations. We celebrate our achievements through balanced and accurate reporting in the media.

. . . we place ourselves in the ecological system, and focus on the well-being of everyone and the earth. We are energy efficient and use renewable energy sources, dramatically slowing the rate of climate change. We only buy what we need, reuse and recycle everything we can, and manufacture sustainably and ethically, so that we live within the capacity of the earth, preserving it for future generations. People everywhere have access to education and healthcare, improving equality, slowing population growth, and further reducing our impact on the earth.

. . . we have healthy forests, farms, waterways, and oceans because we incorporate total land management into our everyday decision making. Everyone around the world participates in the earth's abundance, eating healthy food grown sustainably thanks to our adoption of sustainable farming and fishing policies. Our protection and replanting of forests, and use of sustainable agricultural systems and fishing practices, improves the well-being of all living things, while ensuring that the earth can continue to support us into the future.

. . . the well-being of all living things is high. Our forests are healthy and teeming with wildlife. Previously endangered animals thrive in their natural environments. We create minimal pollution and have new recycling and environmental rehabilitation industries. We live in sustainable urban areas and have laws that protect the environment around the world. We work together through a global network of technology transfer centers to build socially and environmentally sustainable economies, creating strong foundations for future generations.

. . . we have a global economy which supports our individual, collective, and environmental well-being. Governments work together to create the conditions to ensure our economy supports people and the earth through appropriate legislation that protects us both and provides ongoing financial sustainability. With environmental costs incorporated into the prices of goods and services, we are preserving the environment and living within the earth's capacity to support us.

. . . business and governments work together with a common commitment to fiscal, social, and environmental responsibility around the world. Businesses pay their workers fairly for their work, minimize pollution, and look after the environment. Responsible business and financial institutions everywhere are defined by the contribution they make to projects which increase global harmony and environmental sustainability. Because we use an inclusive measure to track our progress, we know exactly how well we are faring financially, socially, and environmentally.

. . . people everywhere have the dignity of being able to support themselves financially through their skills and labor, while living in harmony with the earth. All countries participate equitably in our global economy, agricultural trade is free and fair, and everyone has enough sustainably produced food to eat. Following initial help from improved aid funding and delivery, socially and environmentally sustainable economies thrive across the world. Best of all, we each contributed to this outcome through aid funding, government and private sector involvement, and our participation in the UN. Together, we have increased peace and prosperity for everyone while increasing the well-being of the earth.

We would all like to live in a world like this. That's why working together to create our peaceful planet is so important. Let's make it a reality.

WHAT YOU CAN DO

T here are many ideas in this book about the changes we can make as individuals and together to make our planet a more peaceful place to live. I hope that you have been inspired when reading them, and moved to fulfill this vision in whatever capacity you can.

For every idea in this book, there are thousands more that each of you have, based on your experience, expertise, and knowledge of your part of the world, that can contribute to creating a more harmonious and equitable planet. I encourage you to be creative in building on these ideas, and to use your skills and talents to turn them into reality. It will take our joint efforts in every sphere outlined in this book to create our peaceful planet. I firmly believe that together we can achieve amazing things.

If, however, you feel a bit overwhelmed, I have outlined some actions below that you can take at an individual, community, and world level to contribute to our peaceful planet. All positive change, no matter how small, is significant and contributes cumulatively to a better world.

At the Individual Level
Every one of us can do the exercises in the first three chapters of the book to heal our negative beliefs, use of power and identity, and dominance over the

earth. You are beautiful, important, and you deserve to be happy and at peace. Remember to keep using the exercises until you feel free of pain and peaceful inside. A common response, once you have done the exercises and are feeling happier within yourself, is the desire to reach out and build better relationships with your partner, family, and friends. Spending loving, enjoyable, quality time together increases everyone's well-being. From this basis, we can build strong families and communities, heal our negative collective beliefs, and create a peaceful world.

We can influence the behavior of governments and corporations through our voting and purchasing power. When we are electing leaders, it is up to each of us to vote for those who demonstrate inner peace and inner strength, and who have made a commitment to peace, good governance, and environmental protection. If our leaders are not demonstrating these things, it is up to us to pressure governments to better represent us and our positive beliefs.

The success of people-power ending dictatorships and one-party systems in the Philippines in the 1980s, and in Eastern Europe and Indonesia in the early 1990s, proves that you do have a voice and it will be heard. While demonstrations are one way to enact change, you can also use the internet and social media to support those making positive changes. You can add your weight to community organizations that are advocating governments and corporations for policy changes that create harmony and improve the well-being of all living things.

Those of us in the developed and rapidly developing worlds have a lot of influence through our purchasing power. By changing our purchasing patterns, we can change agricultural and manufacturing processes, driving the growth of environmentally friendly technologies and industries. Producers will respond to growing demand for ethical, clean, quality products.

The first step each of us can take is to consider the impact of our consumption, and identify where we can reduce or shift it. For example, rather than buying four new pairs of shoes each season, the latest version of a gadget you already have, or another cheap toy for your child, donate the money to a charity that helps the environment or people in need. Use it to crowdfund a project that improves harmony and well-being in the world. You can spend the time you would have spent at the shops playing with your children, volunteering in your community, or providing your input into crowdsourcing initiatives that help develop new government policies or environmentally friendly technology.

You can shift your consumption by being mindful of where and how the products you buy have been produced. It is more than likely that a five-dollar, low-quality cotton T-shirt has been made by slave labor in a factory with no environmental controls. By purchasing it, you are contributing to the continuation of slave labor and pollution. So rather than buying four five-dollar T-shirts in different colors that will only last one season because the material is so thin, go to another retail outlet and buy one quality T-shirt for $20. By paying a fair price for the goods we buy, we help ensure that all people are paid fairly for their work and the environment is cared for. In addition to not supporting exploitative and polluting manufacturers, the T-shirt will last longer and you will generate less waste.

We can take this practice one step further by only buying goods and shares from manufacturers who have made public commitments to ethical, environmentally friendly manufacturing, demonstrated through product labeling or other forms of international monitoring. This investment policy can extend to corporations who only engage in creating goods and services which enhance our well-being, as opposed to those which create weapons or destroy rainforests. Your actions will force companies to adopt ethical, clean manufacturing methods and move into more harmonious and environmentally friendly industries, or they will go out of business.

You can also use your purchasing power to look after the environment by:

- buying products made in ways that do not harm the environment, including organic food, clothes made from organic material, sustainably caught fish, green cleaning products, and products made from recycled materials
- buying local, sustainably produced food in season, which supports local farmers and reduces the carbon emissions from transporting the food. Where this is not possible, buying food which has been produced under fair trade principles

- drinking tap water in developed countries, rather than bottled water. Plastic water bottles create unnecessary pollution and waste
- buying products that are not made from wildlife, including shells
- making your home environmentally friendly by introducing energy efficiency measures such as insulation and energy saving light bulbs, and adopting environmental friendly technologies, such as home water recycling systems and solar panels and
- purchasing hybrid cars and electric cars — keeping in mind that electric cars have the least impact on the environment when the electricity has been generated using renewable sources.

You can choose to holiday in places where human rights are respected. Our collective decision not to go to countries where human trafficking, slave labor, or child sex labor is widespread will force the governments of those nations to take action to end these exploitative practices.

If you are wealthy or have a high public profile, I encourage you to use your influence and money to increase the well-being of others and the planet. Remember that happiness does not come from what we have, it comes from inside us and increases when we help others, and help to restore the earth. You can use your business acumen and drive to become directly involved in solving some of the world's problems. Or you can donate large sums of money to non-governmental organizations to deliver specific projects close to your heart.

At the Community Level

You can choose to contribute your time, energy, or funds to projects within your local community to bring about positive change. For example, you can donate your technical or fundraising skills to help your child's school become green by adopting small-scale renewable energy systems and a recycling program. Or you can rehabilitate a local habitat with your neighbors. You can create spaces and activities which bring different groups of people together to build inclusion in your community.

Those who are more articulate can lobby local governments to create the type of environmentally responsible place that we would like to live in, with good public transport options, energy efficient buildings made from recycled materials, and no development in environmentally sensitive areas. Others may lobby your local electricity providers to switch to renewable energy sources. Some of you may like to stand for election in your local government to represent those of us who believe in creating our peaceful planet, and bring about positive change in your area.

At the Group Level

People naturally group together based on common interests, religion, or cultural background. As our personal beliefs change to become based on inclusion, deservedness, and abundance, we can ensure that the negative collective beliefs of the groups we belong to also change. Working from within groups to heal negative collective beliefs and the use of power and identity is very effective. We can take practical steps to eliminate bias against others and limiting practices that repress groups of people such as women, and replace them with policies and practices that promote harmony, respect, and positive relationships with others. As we practice inclusion, we better appreciate one another's strengths and talents. We build networks and the consensus to make the changes that are required at local, national, and international levels to create peace and improve the well-being of us all.

Some of these networks already exist. There are a number of non-governmental organizations doing very important work in creating peace, looking after the environment, and lobbying governments to enact policies and programs that improve the well-being of people and the planet. The International Committee of the Red Cross, Amnesty International, and the World Wildlife Fund are examples of well-known international organizations, but there are also a number of national organizations doing important work in improving the lives of others and the environment. A more comprehensive list can be found at the end of this chapter.

Your participation in the organization of your choice adds weight to their collective voice and helps to bring about positive change in your community, your nation, and the world. You can contribute in the way that best suits your skills, resources, and interests, such as making donations, undertaking administrative or scientific work, developing policies and lobbying government, providing meals to the homeless, or planting trees.

At Work

We can all suggest positive changes in our workplaces, from reducing our impact on the environment to eliminating exploitation in the supply chain. Those in management positions can adopt corporate, social, and environmental responsibility charters, and then systematically identify and improve their governance and business arrangements to ensure that the principles outlined in the charters are met now and into the future.

The entrepreneurs among us can develop environmentally friendly products or join the trend to develop philanthropic businesses which benefit those in need. We can reach out of our workplace and join with other businesses, governments, and non-governmental organizations on initiatives to create our peaceful planet. The more we work together, the more we will achieve. The most important thing is to do work you can be proud of, that will benefit the earth and the people on it for years to come.

If you are a farmer, you can adopt sustainable agricultural systems and become involved in local land care or greening groups, which provide advice and help with rehabilitating your land. You can create wildlife corridors across your property that link areas of forest and bushland across the country for native animals. Others in the agricultural industry can work with chemical manufacturers to phase out dangerous chemicals, and create organic fertilizers and pesticides.

Those of you in leadership positions in every sector have the power and authority to make the most significant changes to create a peaceful planet, and I encourage you to make it your personal commitment to engender as much positive change in your field as you can. Be inspiring in your leadership. This is particularly important for those who hold positions of political leadership. Make it your personal ethos to make decisions which bring the current and future generations of people in your country peace and environmentally sound prosperity. Work with other nations and groups to heal negative beliefs, and repair damaged relationships using the methodology outlined in Chapter 3.

At the National Level

Some of us have the ability and conviction to advocate for positive change at a national level. Others are very good at designing and implementing new government and business policies and programs that build peaceful and environmentally friendly nations. Others can improve the transparency, accountability, and effectiveness of the professions in which we work. All of these make an important contribution to the countries in which we live.

The steps to create peace and prosperity are outlined in Chapters 4, 5, and 10. These actions are applicable for countries that are recovering post-conflict, shifting from other systems of governance to democracy, building their national economy, eradicating corruption, and improving the functioning of democratic structures. The work of individuals and groups within the countries making the change is vital. Your commitment to improving the lives of your countrymen in an environmentally sustainable way is crucially important, and has a ripple effect across your region and the world.

You can contribute from your positions of leadership in government bureaucracies, or you can help to establish a healthy civil society by participating in business, social, environmental, and philanthropy groups. You can play a part in developing media outlets which engage in responsible, accurate, and ethical reporting. All of these functions are necessary in building the social fabric of your nation, ensuring effective democracy and a well-functioning, sustainable economy.

At the International Level

It used to be the case that only a few people, relatively speaking, had influence at the international level. With the spread of the internet and the growth of non-governmental organizations, this is no longer so. Every one of us can have our say and participate in change at the global level. This is a good thing, because creating our peaceful planet is a big goal requiring international cooperation and support to achieve.

Building democracies, reducing arms, and ending the exploitation of people requires a sustained effort from people across all levels of society — from political leaders to law enforcement agents to everyday people living in the societies where injustices are occurring — to contribute to the healing of negative beliefs within their country. International non-governmental organizations also have a role in shaping the reform agenda, monitoring progress, and helping to rehabilitate affected people. As we make progress in creating a more peaceful world, reforming the United Nations as outlined in Chapter 5 will become the logical thing to do.

International environmental protection and rehabilitation is equally important. We can become involved in developing and implementing new international environmental treaties, and rehabilitating the ocean and areas of environmental significance which cross borders. People from a range of sectors and nations can establish and work in health and technology transfer centers to improve the economic, environmental, and human health of developing countries.

Most of these changes cannot be made without international assistance in the form of expertise and funding. Let's support each other to create our peaceful planet. Those of us living in developed countries can make a contribution by supporting aid programs, financially and socially, by volunteering or by being paid for our expertise. There are many international volunteer and knowledge exchange programs already established in which you can participate. For example, you can participate by building the expertise of politicians and government employees, through teacher exchange programs at schools and universities, by helping to develop trade skills in communities, by rehabilitating endangered animals, or undertaking ecological research.

While those with economic skills can become involved in modifying the world economy to ensure that it best supports us and the environment into the future, the support of everyday world citizens is also required. It is up to us to tell our governments that these changes to our international economy are what we want for the world, for governments to be responsive to our wishes, and then to the economic specialists to make it happen.

There are so many ways that you can contribute to building a world where we live in peace and harmony with each other and our environment. I hope you heal your pain so that you live in peace and happiness, and then seek out opportunities to contribute to our planet. Grab them when they present themselves to you. Being actively involved in building a better world increases the happiness and meaning in your life, and is well-worth embracing. And remember, every contribution, no matter how small, counts. You can inspire others with your ideas for positive change by submitting the details of successful projects that you have been involved in to my website www.yasmindavar.com.

Together we will create our peaceful planet.

ACKNOWLEDGMENTS

I have thoroughly enjoyed bringing this book to life. Researching, writing, thinking, editing, going to the occasional forum, and discovering the need to include more chapters, have all been part of the journey.

It was important to me to bring all the components together into an integrated whole. Many have focused on individual pieces of the puzzle, but without acknowledging the interconnectedness of life and recognizing that our beliefs underpin our actions, we could never hope to bring about sustained change to create a peaceful planet.

It is my deepest hope that I have created a robust enough framework that each of you can find your place in it, and can apply it to any situation which requires healing that I may not have mentioned.

While garnering the knowledge on which this book is based has been a lifelong process, the actual process of developing and publishing the book occurred over an eight year period. I am grateful to the Australian Government for allowing me to work part-time so that I could follow my dream.

My thanks also go to my family and friends who all solicitously asked how the book was progressing for what must have seemed like months on end. Thanks also to all those acquaintances who told me that they thought the book was a great idea and they were looking forward to reading it. Your interest and enthusiasm have given me little lifts along the way.

Special thanks go to Bianca Murcutt who reviewed the first draft of the manuscript in its entirety and provided very useful feedback. Bianca, Catherine Seaberg, and Matthew Goodyear helped refine my healing methodology while Simon Nash lent his economics expertise. You all have my deep gratitude.

A heartfelt thanks to Terry Whalin, Angie Kiesling, and the wonderful team at Morgan James Publishing for seeing the potential in this book and helping me to share my message with the people of the world. Thanks to Meaghan Partridge and Emily Kiesling for their careful editing. Thanks also to Michael Ebeling, who made the introduction to Morgan James Publishing even though he is not my agent. Your actions demonstrate your kindness.

Many writers will tell you that writing can be a lonely craft. My decision to bring a dog into my family has been one of the best of my life. My little bundle of black scruffiness lay by my side, sometimes on his back in the sun or by the heater with his paws in the air, hour after hour, day after day, while I tapped away at my keyboard, paused, gazed out the window, checked references, and wrote some more. I am grateful for his devotion.

Appendix

NON-GOVERNMENTAL ORGANIZATIONS

International Humanitarian Organizations

- Amnesty International campaigns on a wide range of issues to protect and defend human rights — from having prisoners of conscience released to pushing governments and corporations to account for violations of human rights. www.amnesty.org

- FairTrade addresses the injustices of conventional trade by requiring companies to pay sustainable prices to farmers and workers in the developing world. www.fairtrade.org.uk

- Human Rights Watch focuses international attention, through investigations and advocacy, to where human rights around the world are violated. www.hrw.org

- International Committee of the Red Cross provides assistance for victims of war and armed violence, and advocates governments to adopt international humanitarian laws. www.icrc.org

- International Crisis Group is committed to preventing and resolving deadly conflict through field analysis, policy prescriptions, and high-level advocacy of policy makers. www.crisisgroup.org
- Medicins Sans Frontieres (Doctors without Borders) provides emergency, independent, medical humanitarian action to people caught in crises around the world. www.msf.org
- Reporters Sans Frontieres (Reporters without Borders) exposes the limits on press freedom and supports journalists who are being persecuted. www.rsf.org
- Transparency International monitors and publicizes corruption in government, politics, business, and civil society to help bring about change. www.transparency.org
- World Vision works with children, families, and communities to overcome poverty and injustice through relief, development, and advocacy. www.wvi.org

International Environmental Organizations

- 350.org is building a global grassroots climate movement that can hold our leaders accountable to the realities of science and the principles of justice. www.350.org
- The Green Belt Movement empowers communities, particularly women, to conserve the environment and improve livelihoods through planting trees. www.greenbeltmovement.org
- Greenpeace acts to change attitudes and behaviors by campaigning to protect and conserve the environment. www.greenpeace.org
- Sea Shepherd Conservation Society takes direct action to expose the destruction of habitat and slaughter of wildlife in the world's oceans. www.seashepherd.org
- TRAFFIC monitors the global wild animal and plant trade to conserve biodiversity and support sustainable development. www.traffic.org
- World Business Council for Sustainable Development is an organization of more than 500 CEOs and senior executives which generate business solutions to global sustainable development issues. www.wbcsd.org

- World Wildlife Fund works to protect the world's most ecologically important regions through conservation, research, and restoration of the environment. www.worldwildlife.org

National Humanitarian Organizations

- Feeding America provides hunger relief through a nationwide network of food banks. www.feedingamerica.org
- Goodwill Industries International helps people in need reach their full potential through learning and the power of work. www.goodwill.org
- Habitat for Humanity builds homes, community, and hope by creating a world where everyone has a decent place to live. www.habitat.org
- The Salvation Army offer services to people in need, including food distribution, disaster relief, rehabilitation centers, anti-human trafficking efforts, and children's programs. www.salvationarmyusa.org

National Environmental Organizations

- American Forests are dedicated to protecting and restoring healthy forest ecosystems. www.americanforests.org
- Environmental Defense Fund tackles urgent threats with practical solutions guided by science and economics. www.edf.org
- The Rainforest Action Network campaigns for forests, their inhabitants, and the natural systems that sustain life by transforming the global marketplace through education, grassroots organizing, and non-violent direct action. www.ran.org
- Worldwatch Institute works to accelerate the transition to a sustainable world that meets human needs through research and outreach that inspire action. www.worldwatch.org

FURTHER READING

While undertaking research for this book, I was inspired by the work of people who have committed their lives to making the world a better place through their area of specialization. I have listed these people and their work below, in the hope that I pique your interest enough for you to follow their work too, and be similarly inspired.

Deepak Chopra
Power, Freedom and Grace: Living from the Source of Lasting Happiness. USA: Amber-Allen Publishing, Inc, 2006.

Paul Collier
War, Guns and Votes: Democracy in Dangerous Places. London: The Bodley Head, 2009.
The Bottom Billion. New York: Oxford University Press, 2007.

Jared Diamond
Collapse: How Societies Choose to Fail or Survive. London: Penguin Books Ltd, 2005.

Harriet Lamb
Fighting the Banana Wars and Other Fairtrade Battles: How We Took on the Corporate Giants to Change the World. London: Ebury Publishing, 2009.

Paul Roberts
The End of Oil: The Decline of the Petroleum Economy and the Rise of a New Energy Order. London: Bloomsbury, 2004.

Jeffrey Sachs
The End of Poverty: How We Can Make it Happen in Our Lifetime. London: Penguin Books, Ltd, 2005.

Stockholm Institute of Peace Research Institute
www.sipri.org
Worldwatch Institute
All of their State of the World Reports
www.worldwatch.org

REFERENCES

Chapter 1 Healing from the Inside Out

1. D. Chopra, *Power, Freedom and Grace: Living from the Source of Lasting Happiness*. USA: Amber-Allen Publishing, Inc, 2006.
2. W. Dwyer, *You'll See It When You Believe It: The Way to Your Personal Transformation*. New York: William Morrow Paperbacks, 2001.
3. D. Chopra, *Power, Freedom and Grace: Living from the Source of Lasting Happiness*.

Chapter 2 Power, Identity, and Relationships

1. D. Chopra, *Power, Freedom and Grace: Living from the Source of Lasting Happiness*. USA: Amber-Allen Publishing, Inc, 2006.

Chapter 3 Collective Healing

1. T. Weiss, *What's Wrong with the United Nations and How to Fix It*. USA: Polity Press, 2009.
2. M. Lowi, *Water and Power: The Politics of a Scarce Resource in the Jordan River Basin*. Cambridge: Cambridge University Press, 1995.

3. J. Diamond, *Collapse: How Societies Choose to Fail or Survive*. London: Penguin Books Ltd, 2005.

4. Aral Sea Foundation, www.aralsea.org.

5. Red List, *Table 1: Numbers of threatened species by major groups of organisms* (1996–2016), www.iucnredlist.org.

6. D. Suzuki, *The Legacy: An Elder's Vision for Our Sustainable Future*. Australia: Allen & Unwin, 2010.

Chapter 4 Creating Peace in Post-conflict Societies

1. For more information about Australia's multiculturalism, see:
   - Department of Social Services, *The People of Australia: Australia's Multicultural Policy*, February 2011, www.dss.gov.au.
   - Radio National, *New Book on Australia's Multicultural Success*. 23 October 2012, www.radioaustralia.net.

2. P. Collier, *War, Guns and Votes: Democracy in Dangerous Places*. London: The Bodley Head, 2009; T. Friedman, *The World Is Flat: A Brief History of the 21ˢᵗ Century*. New York: Farrer, Strauss and Giroux, 2005; His Holiness the 14th Dalai Lama and L. van den Muyzenburg, *The Leader's Way*. New York: Random House Audio Publishing Group, 2008; B. Obama, *The Audacity of Hope*. Melbourne: The Text Publishing Company, 2006.

3. F. Cerletti, "Wading through Difficult Emotions" in *Unarmed Heroes: The Courage to Go Beyond Violence*. UK: Clairview Books, 2004.

4. P. Collier, *War, Guns and Votes: Democracy in Dangerous Places*.

5. T. Weiss, *What's Wrong with the United Nations and How to Fix It*. USA: Polity Press, 2009.

6. P. Collier, *War, Guns and Votes: Democracy in Dangerous Places*.

7. T. Weiss, *What's Wrong with the United Nations and How to Fix It*.

8. P. Collier, *War, Guns and Votes: Democracy in Dangerous Places*.

9. S. Elsworthy, "Prevention and Resolution of Conflicts Using Nonviolent Methods" in *Peace Direct, Unarmed Heroes*.

10. P. Collier, *War, Guns and Votes: Democracy in Dangerous Places*; A. Giddens, *The Third Way and Its Critics*. Cambridge: Polity Press, 2000.

11. P. Collier, *War, Guns and Votes: Democracy in Dangerous Places*.

12. P. Collier, *The Bottom Billion*. New York: Oxford University Press, 2007.

13. P. Collier, *War, Guns and Votes: Democracy in Dangerous Places*.

14. T. Friedman, *The World Is Flat*.

15. P. Collier, *War, Guns and Votes: Democracy in Dangerous Places*.

16. His Holiness the 14th Dalai Lama and L. van den Muyzenburg, *The Leaders Way*; A. Giddens, *The Third Way and Its Critics*.

17. A. Giddens, *The Third Way and Its Critics*.

18. T. Weiss, *What's Wrong with the United Nations and How to Fix It*; J. Sachs, *The End of Poverty*. London: Penguin Books Ltd, 2005.

19. *Nazi Propoganda: 1933–1945*, www.calvin.edu/academic; A. Thompson, *The Media and the Rwanda Genocide*, http://www.idrc.ca/rwandagenocide/.

20. A. Giddens, *The Third Way and Its Critics*.

Chapter 5 Creating Lasting Peace Worldwide

1. International Crisis Group and the US Department of State both have detailed information about governance and human rights. For more information, visit www.crisisgroup.org and www.state.gov.

2. T. Friedman, *The World Is Flat: A Brief History of the 21ˢᵗ Century*. New York: Farrer, Strauss and Giroux, 2005.

3. SIPRI Yearbook 2016, www.sipri.org

4. Ibid.

5. M. Gillis, *Disarmament: A Basic Guide, Third Edition 2012*, www.un.org/disarmament; Organisation for the Prohibition of Chemical Weapons, *Report of the OPCW on the Implementation of the Convention on the Prohibition of the Development, Production, Stockpiling and Use of Chemical Weapons and on their Destruction in 2014*, December 2015, www.opcw.org.

6. M. Gorbachev, *Manifesto for the Earth: Action Now for Peace, Global Justice and a Sustainable Future*. UK: Clairview Books, 2006; R. Green in *Unarmed Heroes: The Courage to Go Beyond Violence*. UK: Clairview Books, 2004.

7. B. McNeil, *The Clean Industrial Revolution*. Australia: Allen & Unwin, 2009; P. Roberts, *The End of Oil: The Decline of the Petroleum Economy and the Rise of a New Energy Order*. London: Bloomsbury, 2004.

8. M. Gillis, *Disarmament: A Basic Guide, Third Edition* 2012; L. O'Donnell, "Nuclear Fallout" in *Australian Magazine*, March 24–25 2001, pp30-34.

9. Ministry of Foreign Affairs, Government of Norway, *Conference: Humanitarian Impact of Nuclear Weapons*, www.regjeringen.no.

10. The International Atomic Energy Agency was established to promote the peaceful uses of nuclear energy and limit the development of nuclear energy for military purposes. It applies safeguards such as monitoring programs in an attempt to ensure that nuclear material and technology is not diverted to the development of weapons. www.iaea.org.

11. B. McNeil, *The Clean Industrial Revolution*.

12. *Fukushima Accident 2011*, www.world-nuclear.org; R. Wallace, "Blast risk mars Fukushima nuclear plant plugging", *The Australian*, 7 April 2011, www.theaustralian.com.au; K. de Freytas-Tamura, "Seafood Radiation hits Japan's Sushi", *The Sydney Morning Herald*, 7 April 2011, www.news.smh. com.au.

13. M. Gorbachev, *Manifesto for the Earth: Action Now for Peace, Global Justice and a Sustainable Future*; R. Wallace, *Fukushima Daiichi danger rating raised to highest, alongside Chernobyl*, 13 April 2011, www.theaustralian. com.au.

14. "Outage hits pumps at Fukushima plant; toxic water leaks into ocean," *The Japan Times*, 21 April 2015, www.japantimes.co.jp; J. McCurray, "Fukushima nuclear clean up enters critical phase," *The Guardian*, 8 November 2013, www.theguardian.com; M. Willacy, "New radiation hotspots found at Fukushima nuclear plant," *ABC News*, 2 September 2013, www.abc.net.au/news; M. Willacy, "Fukushima operators admit radioactive water is leaking into Pacific", *ABC News*, 23 July 2013, www. abc.net.au/news.

15. The Institute for Energy and Environmental Research, *Uranium: Its Uses and Hazards*, www.ieer.org.

16. L. O'Donnell, "Nuclear Fallout."

17. M. Gorbachev, *Manifesto for the Earth: Action Now for Peace, Global Justice and a Sustainable Future*.

18. Transparency International, *Corruption Perceptions Index 2015*, www.transparency.org.

19. Transparency International compile detailed reports on corruption by country and industry. www.transparency.org.

20. S. Rose–Ackerman, "The Challenge of Poor Governance and Corruption" in B. Lomberg, *How to Spend $50 Billion to Make the World a Better Place*. New York: Cambridge University Press, 2006.

21. P. Collier, *The Bottom Billion*. New York: Oxford University Press, 2007.

22. P. Svedberg, "Hunger and Malnutrition: Opponents' Views" in B. Lomberg, *How to Spend $50 Billion to Make the World a Better Place*.

23. P. Collier, *The Bottom Billion*.

24. A. Gore, *Earth in the Balance*. London: Earthscan, 2007.

25. International Labour Organization, *Forced Labour, human trafficking and slavery*, www.ilo.org.

26. United Nations Office on Drugs and Crime, *Global Report on Trafficking in Persons 2014*, www.unodc.org.

27. Ibid.

28. Ibid.

29. Ibid.

30. United Nations Office on Drugs and Crime, *World Drug Report 2010*, www.unodc.org.

31. The United Nations Office on Drugs and Crime releases an annual report which details the extent and impact of the illicit drug market. www.unodc.org.

32. M. Clayfield, "Comment: Notes from el norte: Narco tours, drug lords and the approach to the US border," *SBS News*, 7 January 2015, www.sbs.com.au.

33. United Nations Office on Drugs and Crime, *World Drug Report 2016*, www.unodc.org.

34. Ibid.

35. R. Spencer, "Syria: Russia and US embroiled in row over arms supply," *The Telegraph*, 12 June 2012, www.telegraph.co.uk; R. Gladstone, "Friction at

the UN as Russia and China Veto another Resolution on Syria Sanctions," *The New York Times*, 19 July 2012, www.nytimes.com.

36. L. Rodgers, D. Gritten, J. Offer and P. Asare, "Syria: The story of the conflict," *BBC News*, 9 October 2015, www.bbc.com.

37. *Article 25, Charter of the United Nations*, www.un.org.

Chapter 6 Rethinking Resource Use

1. D. Abram, *The Spell of the Sensuous*. New York: Vintage Books, 1997; E. Assadourian, "The Rise and Fall of Consumer Cultures," in The Worldwatch Institute, *State of the World 2010: Transforming Cultures from Consumerism to Sustainability*. London: Earthscan, 2010; G. Davies, *Economia*. Sydney: ABC Books, 2004; J. Dawson, "Ecovillages and the Transformation of Values," in The Worldwatch Institute, *State of the World 2010: Transforming Cultures from Consumerism to Sustainability*; A. Gore, *Earth in the Balance*. London: Earthscan, 2007.

2. CFCC15 Scientific Committee, *Our Common Future under Climate Change — Outcome Statement*, www.commonfuture-paris2015.org.

3. B. McNeil, *The Clean Industrial Revolution*. Australia: Allen & Unwin, 2009.

4. Intergovernmental Panel on Climate Change, *Climate Change 2007: Synthesis Report*, www.ipcc.ch; M. Renner, "Climate Change and Displacements," in The Worldwatch Institute, *State of the World 2013: Is Sustainability Still Possible?* Washington: Island Press, 2013; A. Sahns and L. Crowder, "Sustainable Fisheries and Seas: Preventing Ecological Collapse," in The Worldwatch Institute, *State of the World 2013: Is Sustainability Still Possible?*

5. United Nations Framework Convention on Climate Change, *Report of the Conference of the Parties on its Sixteenth Session, held in Cancun from 29 November to 10 December 2010*, www.unfccc.int.

6. Australian Alps National Parks, *Climate Change and the Alps*, www.australianalps.environment.gov.au; Australian Government, *The Great Barrier Reef and Climate Change*, www.climatechange.gov.au; A. Gore, *The*

Future; J. Serrill, *Continental shifts in alpine plant ecosystems influenced by climate change,* 11 January 2011, www.labgrab.com.

7. M. Renner, "Climate Change and Displacements," in The Worldwatch Institute, *State of the World 2013: Is Sustainability Still Possible?*

8. Ibid.

9. Intergovernmental Panel on Climate Change, *Climate Change 2007: Synthesis Report,* www.ipcc.ch.

10. M. Gorbachev, *Manifesto for the Earth: Action Now for Peace, Global Justice and a Sustainable Future.* UK: Clairview Books, 2006; M. Renner, "Broadening the Understanding of Security," in The Worldwatch Institute, *State of the World 2010: Transforming Cultures from Consumerism to Sustainability.*

11. Intergovernmental Panel on Climate Change, *Climate Change 2014: Synthesis Report for Policymakers* and *Climate Change 2007: Synthesis Report,* www.ipcc.ch.

12. J. Hansen, "Here comes the sun: chilling verdict on a climate going to extremes," *The Sydney Morning Herald,* 7 August 2012, www.smh.com. au; Intergovernmental Panel on Climate Change, *Climate Change 2014: Synthesis Report for Policymakers,* www.ipcc.ch; The Potsdam Institute for Climate Impact Research and Climate Analysis, *Turn Down the Heat: Why a 4°C Warmer World Must be Avoided, A Report for the World Bank by the Potsdam Institute for Climate Impact Research and Climate Analysis,* 2012; H. Stewart and L. Elliot, "Nicholas Stern: 'I got it wrong on climate change — it's far, far worse,'" *The Guardian,* 26 January 2013, www. guardian.co.uk.

13. The Potsdam Institute for Climate Impact Research and Climate Analysis, *Turn Down the Heat: Why a 4°C Warmer World Must be Avoided, A Report for the World Bank;* M. Gorbachev, *Manifesto for the Earth: Action Now for Peace, Global Justice and a Sustainable Future;* Intergovernmental Panel on Climate Change, *Climate Change 2007: Synthesis Report.*

14. Green Lifestyle Changes, *How much did the US spend on Imported Oil in 2014?* www.greenlifestylechanges.com; US Energy Information

Administration, *Frequently Asked Questions: How much petroleum does the United States import and export?* 4 October 2016, www.eia.gov.

15. P. Collier, *The Bottom Billion*. New York: Oxford University Press, 2007; T. Friedman, *The World Is Flat: A Brief History of the 21ˢᵗ Century*. New York: Farrer, Strauss and Giroux, 2005; B. Obama, *The Audacity of Hope*. Melbourne: The Text Publishing Company, 2006.

16. P. Roberts, *The End of Oil: The Decline of the Petroleum Economy and the Rise of a New Energy Order*. London: Bloomsbury, 2004.

17. P. Saieg, "Energy Efficiency in the Built Environment," in the Worldwatch Institute, *State of the World 2013: Is Sustainability Still Possible?*

18. P. Roberts, *The End of Oil: The Decline of the Petroleum Economy and the Rise of a New Energy Order*.

19. J. Vidal, "Indian coal power plants kill 120,000 people a year, says Greenpeace," *The Guardian*, 10 March 2013, www.guardian.co.uk; P. Galuszka, "China and India Are Building 4 New Coal Power Plants — Every Week," *The New York Times*, 14 November 2012, quoted on The Global Warming Policy Foundation website, www.thegwpf.org; J. Diamond, *Collapse: How Societies Choose to Fail or Survive,* London: Penguin Books Ltd, 2005; P. Roberts *The End of Oil: The Decline of the Petroleum Economy and the Rise of a New Energy Order*.

20. Carbon Tracker and Grantham Research Institute on Climate Change, London School of Economics, *Unburnable Carbon 2013: Wasted capital and stranded assets,* 2013.

21. CSIRO, *Distributed Energy has the Power to Save Billions*, 11 December 2009, www.csiro.au/news.

22. Ibid.

23. B. McNeil, *The Clean Industrial Revolution*; J. Porteous, "Towards baseload solar thermal power," *Ecos Magazine*, 4 May 2011, www.ecosmagazine. com.

24. G. Davies, *Economia*; International Energy Agency, *Fossil Fuel Subsidy Database,* www.worldenergyoutlook.com; B. Obama, *The Audacity of Hope*; P. Roberts, *The End of Oil: The Decline of the Petroleum Economy and*

the Rise of a New Energy Order; N. Stern, *A Blueprint for a Safer Planet*. London: Vintage Books, 2010.

25. Renewable Energy Policy Network for the 21st Century, *REN21 Renewables 2016 Global Status Report*, 1 June 2016, www.ren21.net.

26. B. McNeil, *The Clean Industrial Revolution*.

27. T. Friedman, *The World Is Flat: A Brief History of the 21st Century*; P. Roberts, *The End of Oil: The Decline of the Petroleum Economy and the Rise of a New Energy Order*.

28. B. McNeil, *The Clean Industrial Revolution*.

29. A. Gore, *The Future*.

30. J. Connor, "Reignition: the positive side of Cancun," *Ecos Magazine*, 9 March 2011, www.ecosmagazine.com; S. Mann, "Kyoto retained in climate deal," *The Sydney Morning Herald*, 12 December 2010, www.smh.com.au.

31. L. A. Santos, "For Jeffrey Sachs, the $100B climate finance target has 2 major problems," *Devex*, 4 August 2015, www.devex.com.

32. E. Assadourian, "The Rise and Fall of Consumer Cultures," in The Worldwatch Institute, *State of the World 2010: Transforming Cultures from Consumerism to Sustainability*.

33. Ibid.

34. Ibid.

35. Ibid.

36. Global Footprint Network, *World Footprint: Do we fit on the planet?* www.footprintnetwork.org; E. Assadourian, "The Rise and Fall of Consumer Cultures," in The Worldwatch Institute, *State of the World 2010: Transforming Cultures from Consumerism to Sustainability*.

37. R. Constanza, J. Farley and I. Kubiszewski, "Adapting Institutions for Life in a Full World," in The Worldwatch Institute, *State of the World 2010: Transforming Cultures from Consumerism to Sustainability*.

38. W. McDonough and M Braungart, "Cradle to Cradle: Adapting Production to Nature's Model," in The Worldwatch Institute, *State of the World 2010: Transforming Cultures from Consumerism to Sustainability*.

39. A. Gore, *Earth in the Balance*.

40. P. Collier, *The Bottom Billion*.

41. S. Dechian, "Mapping the impacts of consumer choice," *Ecos Magazine*, Dec–Jan 2011; S. Rooney, "Real-time purchasing power," *Ecos Magazine*, Dec–Jan 2011, www.ecosmagazine.com. GoodGuide is at www.goodguide. com, and Sourcemap is at www.sourcemap.org.

42. J. Diamond, *Collapse: How Societies Choose to Fail or Survive*.

43. M. Maniates, "Editing out Unsustainable Behavior," in The Worldwatch Institute, *State of the World 2010: Transforming Cultures from Consumerism to Sustainability*.

44. E. Assadourian, "The Rise and Fall of Consumer Cultures," in The Worldwatch Institute, *State of the World 2010: Transforming Cultures from Consumerism to Sustainability*.

45. J. Diamond, *Collapse: How Societies Choose to Fail or Survive*.

46. Ibid.

47. United Nations, *World population projected to reach 9.6 billion by 2050 with most growth in developing regions, especially Africa — says UN*, 13 June 2013, www.un.org; Worldometers, *Current World Population*, www. worldometers.info, accessed 27 November 2015.

48. A. Gore, *Earth in the Balance*.

49. J. Sachs, *The End of Poverty: How We Can Make it Happen in Our Lifetime*. London: Penguin Books, Ltd, 2005.

Chapter 7 Feeding Everyone Sustainably

1. Institution of Mechanical Engineers, *Global Food: Waste Not, Want Not*, 10 January 2013, www.imeche.org; World Food Programme, *Hunger Statistics*, www.wfp.org.

2. G. Kissinger, M. Herold, and V. de Sy, *Drivers of Deforestation and Forest Degradation: A Synthesis Report for REDD+ Policymakers*, 2012, www. decc.gov.uk; Calculation based on an estimated 8.8 million hectares of deforestation per year between 2010 and 2015, Food and Agriculture Organization of the United Nations, *Global Forest Resources Assessment 2015: How are the world's forests changing*, www.fao.org.

3. Food and Agriculture Organization of the United Nations, *Global Forest Resources Assessment 2015: How are the world's forests changing*, www.fao.org.

4. A. Gore, *The Future*. UK: WH Allen, 2014.

5. *Glossary of Environmental Statistics, Studies in Methods*, Series F, No. 67, United Nations, New York, 1997, quoted in Organisation for Economic and Co-operation and Development, *Glossary of Statistical Terms*, www. oecd.org.

6. D. Suzuki, *The Legacy: An Elder's Vision for Our Sustainable Future*. Australia: Allen & Unwin, 2010.

7. CSIRO, "Call for action on world soil crisis," *The Land*, 18 November 2012, www.theland.com.au.

8. V. Heffernan, *What Farmers Need Forum 2011: Proceedings*. Greening Australia, 2011.

9. T. Rinaudo, P. Dettmann, and A. Tofu, "Carbon trading, community forestry and development: Potential, challenges and the way forward in Ethiopia," *Responses to Poverty 2008*, www.worldvision.com.au; *Carbon Farming Initiative*, www.climatechange.gov.au.

10. V. Heffernan, *What Farmers Need Forum 2011: Proceedings*. Greening Australia, 2011.

11. A. Bates and T. Hemenway, "From Agriculture to Permaculture," in The Worldwatch Institute, *State of the World 2010: Transforming Cultures from Consumerism to Sustainability*, London: Earthscan, 2010.

12. W. Reid et al, *Ecosystems and Human Well-Being: Synthesis, A Report of the Millennium Ecosystem Assessment*, 2005, www.unep.org.

13. Food and Agriculture Organization of the United Nations, *Fertilizer Use to Surpass 200 Million Tonnes in 2018*, 16 February 2015, www.fao.org.

14. D. Suzuki, *The Legacy: An Elder's Vision for Our Sustainable Future*.

15. A. Bates and T. Hemenway, "From Agriculture to Permaculture," in The Worldwatch Institute, *State of the World 2010: Transforming Cultures from Consumerism to Sustainability*.

16. A. Gore, *The Future*. UK: WH Allen, 2014.

17. J. Mair and K. Ganly, "Social Entrepreneurs: Innovation toward Sustainability," in The Worldwatch Institute, *State of the World 2010: Transforming Cultures from Consumerism to Sustainability*; SITA Organics, *The Art of Organics: Making the Planet Sustainable*, www.sita.com.au.

18. G. Davies, *Economia*. Sydney: ABC Books, 2004.

19. A. Gore, *Earth in the Balance*. London: Earthscan, 2007.

20. T. Juniper, *How Many Lightbulbs Does it Take to Change a Planet?* London: Quercus, 2007.

21. Ibid.

22. G. Davies, *Economia*.

23. Food and Agricultural Organization of the United Nations, *Coping with water scarcity: An action framework for agriculture and food security*. Rome, 2012. www.fao.org.

24. S. Postel, "Sustaining Freshwater and Its Dependents," in The Worldwatch Institute, *State of the World 2013: Is Sustainability Still Possible?*

25. S. Wenzlau, *Cities Can Work with Farmers to Meet Growing Need for Water*, The Worldwatch Institute, September 2013, www.blogs.worldwatch.org.

26. Institution of Mechanical Engineers, *Global Food: Waste Not, Want Not*.

27. World Health Organization, *Obesity and Overweight: Fact Sheet*, June 2016, www.who.int.

28. *A Bloody Business*, Four Corners, 30 May 2011, www.abc.net.au.

29. National Farmers Federation, *Joint industry statement: live export trade recommencement*, 6 July 2011, www.nff.org.au.

30. *Footage reveals horror of Pakistani slaughter*, ABC News, 5 November 2012, www.abc.net.au; *Government releases Indonesian Abattoir Report*, ABC News, 18 May 2012, www.abc.net.au.

31. R. Schiffman, "Are the Oceans Failed States?" *Foreign Policy*, 8 July 2014, www.foreignpolicy.com.

32. A. Sahns and L. Crowder, "Sustainable Fisheries and Seas: Preventing Ecological Collapse," in The Worldwatch Institute, *State of the World 2013: Is Sustainability Still Possible?*; R. Schiffman, "Are the Oceans Failed States?" *Foreign Policy*, 8 July 2014, www.foreignpolicy.com; D. Suzuki, *The Legacy: An Elder's Vision for Our Sustainable Future*.

33. A. Sahns and L. Crowder, "Sustainable Fisheries and Seas: Preventing Ecological Collapse," in The Worldwatch Institute, *State of the World 2013: Is Sustainability Still Possible?*

34. Marine Resources and Fisheries Consultants and Department for International Development, *Policy Brief 9: Fisheries and Subsidies*, 2008, www.mrag.co.uk.

35. Food and Agriculture Organization of the United Nations, *The State of World Fisheries and Aquaculture 2016: Contributing to Food Security and Nutrition for All*, www.fao.org; T. Juniper, *How Many Lightbulbs does it Take to Change a Planet?*

36. Ibid.

37. A. Sahns and L. Crowder, "Sustainable Fisheries and Seas: Preventing Ecological Collapse," in The Worldwatch Institute, *State of the World 2013: Is Sustainability Still Possible?*

38. J. Diamond, *Collapse: How Societies Choose to Fail or Survive.*

39. R. J. Diaz and R. Rosenberg, "Spreading dead zones and consequences for marine ecosystems," *Science*, 321(5891): 926-9, 15 August 2008, www.sciencemag.org; M. Bruckner, *The Gulf of Mexico Dead Zone*, www.serc.carlton.edu.

40. D. Suzuki, *The Legacy: An Elder's Vision for Our Sustainable Future.*

41. World Food Programme, *Hunger Statistics*, www.wfp.org; K. Deininger, D. Byerlee, J. Lindsay, A. Norton, H. Selod, and M. Stickler, *Rising Global Interest in Farmland: Can it Yield Sustainable and Equitable Benefits?*

42. Institution of Mechanical Engineers, *Global Food: Waste Not, Want Not.*

43. Ibid.

44. Ibid.

45. World Food Programme, *Hunger Statistics*, www.wfp.org.

46. "Global food price crisis," *Focus: The Magazine of Australia's Overseas Aid Program*, Volume 26 No 2, June–Sept 2011; B. McNeil, *The Clean Industrial Revolution*. Australia: Allen & Unwin, 2009; M. Renner, "Climate Change and Displacements," in The Worldwatch Institute, *State of the World 2013: Is Sustainability Still Possible?* Washington: Island Press, 2013.

47. "Global food price crisis," *Focus: The Magazine of Australia's Overseas Aid Program.*

48. A. Gore, *The Future*. UK: WH Allen, 2014; D. Nierenberg, "Agriculture: Growing Food–and Solutions," in The Worldwatch Institute, *State of the World 2013: Is Sustainability Still Possible?*; S. Wenslau, *Global Food Prices Continue to Rise*, 11 April 2013, www.worldwatch.org.

49. D. Nabarro, "Ensuring food security for all," *Focus: The Magazine of Australia's Overseas Aid Program*, Volume 26 No 2, June–Sept 2011.

50. K. Deininger, D. Byerlee, J. Lindsay, A. Norton, H. Selod, and M. Stickler, *Rising Global Interest in Farmland: Can it Yield Sustainable and Equitable Benefits?* 2010, www.sitesources.worldbank.org.

51. Institution of Mechanical Engineers, *Global Food: Waste Not, Want Not*; D. Nierenberg, "Agriculture: Growing Food – and Solutions," in The Worldwatch Institute, *State of the World 2013: Is Sustainability Still Possible?*

52. D. Williams, *World Food*, Institute of Mechanical Engineers, August 2011, www.imeche.org.

53. K. Deininger, D. Byerlee, J. Lindsay, A. Norton, H. Selod, and M. Stickler, *Rising Global Interest in Farmland: Can it Yield Sustainable and Equitable Benefits?*; D. Nierenberg, "Agriculture: Growing Food–and Solutions," in The Worldwatch Institute, *State of the World 2013: Is Sustainability Still Possible?*; UN Department of Economic and Social Affairs, *World Economic and Social Survey 2011: The Great Green Technological Transformation*, 2011, www.un.org; D. Williams, *World Food*.

54. D. Nabarro, "Ensuring food security for all," *Focus: The Magazine of Australia's Overseas Aid* Program; UN Department of Economic and Social Affairs, *World Economic and Social Survey 2011: The Great Green Technological Transformation*.

55. Worldwatch Institute, *Land "Grabbing" Grows as Agricultural Resources Dwindle*, 6 October 2015, www.worldwatch.org.

56. Millennium Ecosystem Assessment, *Ecosystems and Human Wellbeing: Synthesis*, 2005, www.unep.org.

57. H. K. Gibbs, M. Johnson, J. A. Foley, T. Holloway, C. Monfreda, N. Ramankutty, D. Zaks, "Carbon payback times for crop-based biofuels expansion in the tropics: the effects of changing yield and technology," *Environmental Research Letters*, Volume 3, No 3, 2008, www.iopscience.

iop.org; B. McNeil, *The Clean Industrial Revolution*; B. Phalen, "Biofuel crops: food security must come first," *The Guardian*, 30 August 2013, www.theguardian.com.

58. T. Juniper, *How Many Lightbulbs Does it Take to Change a Planet?*

Chapter 8 Healing the Earth

1. The IUCN Red List of Threatened Species, *Table 1: Numbers of threatened species by major groups of organisms* (1996-2016), www.iucnredlist.org.

2. N. Skinner, "African elephant numbers collapsing," *Nature: International weekly journal of science*, 19 August 2014, www.nature.com; J. Bonello, *UN recognizes severity of wildlife crimes*, 26 April 2013, www.worldwildlife.org; World Wildlife Fund, Environmental Investigation Agency and TRAFFIC, *Wildlife and Forest Crime: Briefing Document for the United Nations Commission on Crime Prevention and Criminal Justice*, 21 April 2013, www.traffic.org.

3. J. Bonello, *UN recognizes severity of wildlife crimes*, 26 April 2013, www.worldwildlife.org; World Wildlife Fund, Environmental Investigation Agency and TRAFFIC, *Wildlife and Forest Crime: Briefing Document for the United Nations Commission on Crime Prevention and Criminal Justice*, 21 April 2013, www.traffic.org.

4. TRAFFIC: the wildlife trade-monitoring network, *Our Work*, www.traffic.org.

5. B. Dulgnan, *Traditional Chinese Medicine and Endangered Animals*, 22 October 2007, www.advocacy.brittanica.com.

6. Nguyen Dao Ngoc Van and Nguyen Tap, *An Overview of the Use of Plants and Animals in Traditional Medicine Systems in Vietnam: A TRAFFIC Southeast Asia Report*, 2008, www. traffic.org.

7. TRAFFIC, *INTERPOL targets illegal trade in wildlife medical products*, 5 March 2010, www.traffic.org.

8. For more information about research into the use of endangered species in traditional medicine, visit the websites of the World Wildlife Fund at www.worldwildlife.org and TRAFFIC at www.traffic.org.

9. S. Martin, *Paper Chase*, 2011, www.ecology.com.

10. United Nations Framework Convention on Climate Change, *Investment and financial flows to address climate change*, 2007.

11. World Wildlife Fund, Environmental Investigation Agency and TRAFFIC, *Wildlife and Forest Crime: Briefing Document for the United Nations Commission on Crime Prevention and Criminal Justice*, 21 April 2013, www.traffic.org.

12. S. Martin, *Paper Chase.*

13. INTERPOL, *Trade in illegal timber target of INTERPOL and WCO-supported operation in Peru*, 25 July 2014, and *Latin American Countries in first INTERPOL operation against illegal logging*, 19 February 2013, www.interpol.int.

14. Worldwatch Institute, *Paper Production Levels Off, Environmental Footprint Still High*, 20 January 2015, www.worldwatch.org.

15. A. Giddens, *The Third Way and Its Critics*, Cambridge: Polity Press, 2000.

16. W. McDonough and M Braungart, "Cradle to Cradle: Adapting Production to Nature's Model," in The Worldwatch Institute, *State of the World 2010: Transforming Cultures from Consumerism to Sustainability.* London: Earthscan, 2010.

17. A. Gore, *Earth in the Balance*, London: Earthscan, 2007.

18. T. Juniper, *How Many Lightbulbs Does it Take to Change a Planet?* London: Quercus, 2007.

19. C. Cullinan, "Earth Jurisprudence: From Colonization to Participation," in The Worldwatch Institute, *State of the World 2010: Transforming Cultures from Consumerism to Sustainability, 27th edition.* London: Earthscan, 2010.

20. A. Gore, *Earth in the Balance.* London: Earthscan, 2007.

21. His Holiness the 14th Dalai Lama and L. van den Muyzenburg, *The Leader's Way*, New York: Random House Audio Publishing Group, 2008; J. Diamond, *Collapse: How Societies Choose to Fail or Survive.* London: Penguin Books Ltd, 2005.

22. M. Renner, "Broadening the Understanding of Security," in The Worldwatch Institute, *State of the World 2010: Transforming Cultures from Consumerism to Sustainability, 27th edition.* London: Earthscan, 2010.

Chapter 9 Greening Economics

1. His Holiness the 14th Dalai Lama and L. van den Muyzenburg, *The Leader's Way*. New York: Random House Audio Publishing Group, 2008; G. Davies, *Economia*. Sydney: ABC Books, 2004.

2. J. Stanford, *Economics for Everyone: A Short Guide to the Economics of Capitalism*. London and New York: Pluto Press, 2008.

3. B.D. Proctor, J.L. Semega and M.A. Kollar, *Income and Poverty in the United States: 2015*, 13 September 2016, www.census.gov.

4. R. Constanza, G. Alperovitz, H. Daly, J. Farley, C. Franco, T. Jackson, I. Kubiszewski, J. Schor and P. Victor, "Building a Sustainable and Desirable Economy-in-Society-in-Nature," in The Worldwatch Institute, *State of the World 2013: Is Sustainability Still Possible?*, Washington: Island Press, 2013; D. Suzuki, *The Legacy: An Elder's Vision for Our Sustainable Future*, Australia: Allen & Unwin, 2010.

5. R. Constanza, G. Alperovitz, H. Daly, J. Farley, C. Franco, T. Jackson, I. Kubiszewski, J. Schor and P. Victor, "Building a Sustainable and Desirable Economy-in-Society-in-Nature," in The Worldwatch Institute, *State of the World 2013: Is Sustainability Still Possible?*; R. Constanza, J. Farley, and I. Kubiszewski, "Adapting Institutions for Life in a Full World," in The Worldwatch Institute, *State of the World 2010: Transforming Cultures from Consumerism to Sustainability*. London: Earthscan, 2010; M. Göpel, "Guarding our Future: How to Protect Future Generations," *Solutions*, Volume 1, Issue 6: Jan 06, 2011, www.thesolutionsjournal.com; G. Davies, *Economia*. Sydney: ABC Books, 2004; A. Gore, *Earth in the Balance*. London: Earthscan, 2007; J. E. Stiglitz, A. Sen, and J. Fitoussi, *Report by the Commission on the Measurement of Economic Performance and Social Progress*, 2009, www.stiglitz-sen-fitoussi.fr; D. Suzuki, *The Legacy: An Elder's Vision for Our Sustainable Future*.

6. R. Constanza, G. Alperovitz, H. Daly, J. Farley, C. Franco, T. Jackson, I. Kubiszewski, J. Schor and P. Victor, "Building a Sustainable and Desirable Economy-in-Society-in-Nature," in The Worldwatch Institute, *State of the World 2013: Is Sustainability Still Possible?*; R. Constanza, J. Farley, and I. Kubiszewski, "Adapting Institutions for Life in a Full World," in

The Worldwatch Institute, *State of the World 2010: Transforming Cultures from Consumerism to Sustainability.* London: Earthscan, 2010; T. Dean, "Dethroning GDP as our measure of progress," *The Drum*, 16 January 2014, www.abc.net.au; A. Gore, *Earth in the Balance.* London: Earthscan, 2007.

7. A. Gore, *Earth in the Balance.*

8. T. Juniper, *How Many Lightbulbs Does it Take to Change a Planet?* London: Quercus, 2007; N. Stern, *A Blueprint for a Safer Planet.* London: Vintage Books, 2010; D. Suzuki, *The Legacy: An Elder's Vision for Our Sustainable Future.*

9. Citizens for Tax Justice, *Offshore Shell Games 2016: The Use of Offshore Tax Havens by Fortune 500 Companies,* 4 October 2016, www.ctj.org.

10. AFL-CIO, *CEO Pay and Corporate Income Tax Avoidance,* www.aflcio.org.

11. G. Davies, *Economia*; J. Stanford, *Economics for Everyone: A Short Guide to the Economics of Capitalism.*

12. D. Suzuki, *The Legacy: An Elder's Vision for Our Sustainable Future.*

13. G. Davies, *Economia*; A. Gore, *The Future.* UK: WH Allen, 2014.

14. A. Gore, *The Future.*

15. J. Sachs, *The Price of Civilization: Economics and Ethics After the Fall.* London: The Bodley Head, 2011.

16. "Big Three Spending Millions on Lobbying," *CBS News*, 26 May 2009, www.cbsnews.com.

17. B. McNeil, *The Clean Industrial Revolution.* Australia: Allen & Unwin, 2009.

18. "President Barack Obama says that after bailout, GM is now the world's top automaker," *Tampa Bay Times*, 25 January 2012, www.politifact.com.

19. K. Amadeo, "The Auto Industry Bailout: Why GM, Ford and Chrysler Asked for Government Loans," *about.com*, 12 January 2013, www.useconomy.about.com.

20. M. Gongloff, "Banks Could Still Blow Up the World," *The Huffington Post*, 22 January 2014, www.huffingtonpost.com.au.

21. A. Gore, *The Future*. UK: WH Allen, 2014; M. Sivy, "Why Derivatives May Be the Biggest Risk for the Global Economy," *Time*, 27 March 2013, www.business.time.com.

22. Ibid.

23. P. Roberts, *The End of Oil: The Decline of the Petroleum Economy and the Rise of a New Energy Order*. London: Bloomsbury, 2004.

24. M. Gorbachev, *Manifesto for the Earth: Action Now for Peace, Global Justice and a Sustainable Future*. UK: Clairview Books, 2006; B. McNeil, *The Clean Industrial Revolution*; J. Stanford, *Economics for Everyone: A Short Guide to the Economics of Capitalism*.

25. A. Giddens, *The Third Way and Its Critics*. Cambridge: Polity Press, 2000; B. Obama, *The Audacity of Hope*. Melbourne: The Text Publishing Company, 2006; J. Stanford, *Economics for Everyone: A Short Guide to the Economics of Capitalism*.

26. J. Sachs, *The Price of Civilization: Economics and Ethics After the Fall*.

27. Ibid.

28. T. Juniper, *How Many Lightbulbs Does it Take to Change a Planet?*

29. J. Stanford, *Economics for Everyone: A Short Guide to the Economics of Capitalism*.

30. A. Gore, *Earth in the Balance*; T. Juniper, *How Many Lightbulbs Does it Take to Change a Planet?*

31. J. Hohensee, "Corporate Reporting and Externalities," in The Worldwatch Institute, *State of the World 2013: Is Sustainability Still Possible?*

32. J. Sachs, *The Price of Civilization: Economics and Ethics After the Fall*.

33. J. Diamond, *Collapse: How Societies Choose to Fail or Survive*. London: Penguin Books Ltd, 2005; B. McNeil, *The Clean Industrial Revolution*.

34. His Holiness the 14th Dalai Lama and L. van den Muyzenburg, *The Leader's Way*; B. McNeil, *The Clean Industrial Revolution*; S. Rooney, "Real-time purchasing power," *Ecos*, Dec–Jan 2011, www.ecosmagazine.com.

35. United Nations Global Compact, *UN Global Compact Infographic*, 2015, www.unglobalcompact.org; T. Weiss, *What's Wrong with the United Nations and How to Fix It*. USA: Polity Press, 2009.

Chapter 10 Equalizing Economics

1. The World Bank, *Poverty and Equity Database*, www.databank.worldbank. org.

2. C. Dunmore, "Farm subsidies still get top share of EU austerity budget," *Reuters*, 8 February 2013, www.reuters.com; Environmental Working Group, "The United States Summary Information," www.farm.ewg.org; G. Potter, "Agricultural Subsidies Remain a Staple in the Industrial World," *Vital Signs*, 28 February 2014, www.vitalsigns.worldwatch.org.

3. Based on a total figure of $32.9 billion in subsidies for cotton between 1995 and 2012, adjusted for inflation, Environmental Working Group, "Top Programs in the United States." www.farm.ewg.org.

4. H. Lamb, *Fighting the Banana Wars* and *Other Fairtrade Battles: How We Took on the Corporate Giants to Change the World*. London: Ebury Publishing, 2009.

5. J. M. Alston, D.A. Sumner, and H. Brunke, *Impacts of Reductions in US Cotton Subsidies on West African Cotton Producers*. Boston: Oxfam America, 2007. www.oxfamamerica.org.

6. Environmental Working Group, "The United States Summary Information." www.farm.ewg.org.

7. N. Nielsen, "EU farm subsidies remain cloaked in secrecy," *EUobserver*, 10 May 2012, www.euobserver.com.

8. G. Davies, *Economia*. Sydney: ABC Books, 2004; T. Juniper, *How Many Lightbulbs Does it Take to Change a Planet?* London: Quercus, 2007.

9. A. Gore, *Earth in the Balance*. London: Earthscan, 2007.

10. The World Bank, *International Debt Statistics 2016*, Washington DC, www. data.worldbank.org.

11. S. Gutterman, "Putin says Russia seeking IMF reform, battling offshores," 13 June 2013, *Reuters*, www.reuters.com; J. Sachs, *The End of Poverty: How We Can Make it Happen in Our Lifetime*. London: Penguin Books, 2005.

12. ECA Watch, *What are ECAs?* www.eca-watch.org; T. Juniper, *How Many Lightbulbs Does it Take to Change a Planet?*

13. P. Collier, *The Bottom Billion*. New York: Oxford University Press, 2007; T. Juniper, *How Many Lightbulbs Does it Take to Change a Planet?*

14. G. Davies, *Economia*; T. Juniper, *How Many Lightbulbs Does it Take to Change a Planet?*; United Nations Department of Economic and Social Affairs, *World Economic and Social Survey 2011: The Great Green Technological Transformation*. New York, 2011.

15. T. Juniper, *How Many Lightbulbs Does it Take to Change a Planet?*; J. Sachs, *The End of Poverty: How We Can Make it Happen in Our Lifetime*.

16. P. Collier, *The Bottom Billion*.

17. Organisation for Economic Cooperation and Development, *Development aid stable in 2014 but flows to poorest countries still falling*, 8 April 2015, www.oecd.org.

18. G. Potter, "Agricultural Subsidies Remain a Staple in the Industrial World," *Vital Signs*, 28 February 2014, www.vitalsigns.worldwatch.org.

19. A. Shah, *Foreign Aid for Development Assistance*, 28 September 2014, www. globalissues.org.

20. Ibid.

21. "Dire Shortage at UN Food Agency," *BBC News*, 31 July 2009, www. bbc.co.uk; "AP Interview: Head of World Food Programme says funding outlook for Syrian refugees is 'bleak,'" *Fox News*, 11 August 2015, www. foxnews.com.

22. J. Sachs, *The End of Poverty: How We Can Make it Happen in Our Lifetime*.

23. Oxfam, *Make Poverty History and G8 promises — was it all really worth it?* 30 May 2013, www.oxfam.org.uk.

24. K. McNeill, D. Doane, and G. Tarman, "The lessons from Make Poverty History," 31 May 2012, *The Guardian*, www.theguardian.com; The World Bank, *International Debt Statistics 2016*, Washington DC, www. openknowledge.worldbank.org.

25. T. Juniper *How Many Lightbulbs Does it Take to Change a Planet?*; H. Lamb, *Fighting the Banana Wars* and *Other Fairtrade Battles: How We Took on the Corporate Giants to Change the World*; J. Sachs, *The End of Poverty: How We Can Make it Happen in Our Lifetime*.

26. International Monetary Fund, *Debt Relief under the Heavily Indebted Poor Countries (HIPC) Initiative*, 2 April 2013, www.imf.org.

27. Oxfam, *Make Poverty History and G8 promises — was it all really worth it?* 30 May 2013, www.oxfam.org.uk.

28. J. Tobin, "A Proposal for International Monetary Reform," *Eastern Economics Journal*, 1978, 4(3-4): 153-159, available at www.ideas.repec. org.

29. Investor Guide, *Understanding the Risks of Currency Speculation*, 25 January 2013, www.investorguide.com.

30. J. Tobin, "A Proposal for International Monetary Reform," *Eastern Economics Journal*, 1978, 4(3-4): 153-159, available at www.globalpolicy. org.

31. Based on a daily rate of $4.4 trillion and 260 trading days per year, The City UK, *London increases its lead in foreign exchange trading as global turnover drops 7 percent*, 29 January 2013, www.thecityuk.com.

32. J. Sachs, *The End of Poverty: How We Can Make it Happen in Our Lifetime.*

33. Ibid.

ABOUT THE AUTHOR

 Yasmin Davar was inspired at a young age to undertake work that makes a positive difference in the world. She is an environmental engineer with a Master of International Studies in Peace and Conflict Resolution and training in Corporate Governance. In the last 20 years, Yasmin has introduced positive reforms to policies and programs in academia, business and government while undertaking her personal healing journey and helping others with theirs. She lives in Sydney, Australia.

Morgan James Speakers Group

www.TheMorganJamesSpeakersGroup.com

We connect Morgan James published authors with live and online events and audiences whom will benefit from their expertise.

Morgan James makes all of our titles available
through the Library for All Charity Organizations.

www.LibraryForAll.org

Printed in the USA
CPSIA information can be obtained
at www.ICGtesting.com
JSHW022336140824
68134JS00019B/1516